# FOUNDATIONS
## OLD TESTAMENT
### A 260-DAY BIBLE READING PLAN FOR BUSY BELIEVERS

Lifeway Press® • Nashville, Tennessee

Hamilton Barber
*Writer*

Susan Hill
*Content Editor*

Jon Rodda
*Art Director*

Joel Polk
*Editorial Team Leader*

Brian Daniel
*Manager, Short-Term Discipleship*

Brandon Hiltibidal
*Director, Groups Ministry*



ISBN 978-1-0877-4170-3 • Item 005831469

Dewey decimal classification: 220.07
Subject headings: BIBLE. O.T.--STUDY AND TEACHING / BIBLE. O.T.--READING / DISCIPLESHIP



To order additional copies of this resource, write to Lifeway Resources Customer Service; One Lifeway Plaza; Nashville, TN 37234; fax 615-251-5933; phone toll free 800-458-2772; email orderentry@lifeway.com; or order online at Lifeway.com.

*Printed in the United States of America*

Groups Ministry Publishing • Lifeway Resources
One Lifeway Plaza • Nashville, TN 37234

# Contents

# ABOUT THE AUTHORS

**ROBBY GALLATY** is the senior pastor of Long Hollow Baptist Church in Hendersonville, Tennessee. He was radically saved from a life of drug and alcohol addiction on November 12, 2002. In 2008 he founded Replicate Ministries to educate, equip, and empower men and women to be disciples who make disciple makers (replicate.org). He's the author of *Growing Up: How to Be a Disciple Who Makes Disciples* (B&H, 2013), *The Forgotten Jesus: How Western Christians Should Follow an Eastern Rabbi* (Zondervan, 2017), *Rediscovering Discipleship: Making Jesus' Final Words Our First Work* (Zondervan, 2015), and *Here and Now: Thriving in the Kingdom of Heaven Today* (B&H, 2019). He's the coauthor with his wife, Kandi, of *Foundations: A 260-Day Bible Reading Plan for Busy Believers* (Lifeway, 2015).

**KANDI GALLATY** has been investing in the lives of women for over a decade. She believes there are three major sources to draw from when investing in the lives of others: God's Word, God's work in one's life, and God's Spirit. She's passionate about cultivating a biblical worldview from the truths of Scripture and about teaching women how to steward the life experiences and lessons God has allowed in their lives. Together Kandi and Robby lead Replicate Ministries. Kandi loves being a pastor's wife and serving alongside her husband at Long Hollow Baptist Church. Kandi and Robby are the proud, thankful parents of two boys, Rig and Ryder. Kandi is the author of *Disciple Her: Using the Word, Work, and Wonder of God to Invest in Women* (B&H, 2019) and the coauthor with Robby of *Foundations: A 260-Day Bible Reading Plan for Busy Believers* (LifeWay, 2015).

**HAMILTON BARBER** Hamilton is a writer and editor from Hendersonville, TN who serves as the Content Specialist at Long Hollow. He has written several book-length studies, authored articles, and collaborated on projects with authors like Robby Gallaty, Ben Trueblood, Brent Crowe, and Brock Gill. He has found that listening for God's voice most often starts in silence--and in the reading of God's Word. An avid indoorsman, when he isn't working, you can usually find him picking up a new skill he will never have to use.

# INTRODUCTION

When I (Robby) was a new believer, I used the OPRA technique for reading the Bible: I randomly *opened* the Bible, *pointed* to a passage, *read* the verse, and tried to figure out a way to *apply* it to my life. Thankfully, I didn't land on the Scripture that says, "He [Judas Iscariot] went and hanged himself" (Matt 27:5). Reading random Scriptures won't provide solid biblical growth any more than eating random foods from your pantry will provide solid physical growth. An effective reading plan is required.

My wife, Kandi, and I, along with the help of Tim LaFleur and Gus Hernandez, have developed a reading plan called the Foundations 260 Old Testament. The F-260 OT is a 260-day reading plan that covers one chapter a day. In addition, the plan suggests an additional chapter to read if you choose. After using the original Foundations reading plan, we wanted to create an alternative plan that would help provide variety and be more easily digested by new believers.

The plan expects believers to read one chapter a day for five days each week, with an allowance for weekends off. The two off days a week are built in so that you can catch up on days when you're unable to read. With a traditional reading plan of four to five chapters a day, unread chapters can begin to pile up, forcing you to skip entire sections to get back on schedule. It reduces Bible reading to a system of box checking instead of a time to hear from God. The required reading also makes it difficult to sit and reflect on what you've read for that day.

The F-260 OT encourages believers to digest more of the Word by reading less and by keeping a HEAR journal.

### HOW DO I LOG A HEAR JOURNAL ENTRY?

The HEAR journaling method promotes reading the Bible with a life-transforming purpose. No longer will you focus on checking off the boxes on your daily reading schedule; instead, your purpose will be to understand and respond to God's Word.

The acronym HEAR stands for *highlight*, *explain*, *apply*, and *respond*. Each of these four steps helps create an atmosphere to hear God speak. After establishing a place and a time to study God's Word each day, you'll be ready to hear from God.

For an illustration let's assume that you begin your quiet time in the Book of 2 Timothy and that today's reading is chapter 1 of the book. Before reading the text, pause to sincerely ask God to speak to you. It may seem trite, but it's absolutely imperative that we seek God's guidance in order to understand His Word (see 1 Cor. 2:12-14). Every time we open our Bibles, we should pray the simple prayer that David prayed:

*Open my eyes so that I may contemplate*
*wondrous things from your instruction [Word]* (Ps. 119:18).

After praying for the Holy Spirit's guidance, you'll be ready to record your notes. At the end of each day's entry, we have provided a place for you to write your HEAR journal. This exercise will remind you to read with a purpose. In the course of your reading, one or two verses will usually stand out and speak to you. After reading the passage of Scripture, *highlight* each verse that speaks to you by copying it under the letter H. Record the following.

- The name of the book
- The passage of Scripture
- The chapter and verse numbers that especially speak to you
- A title to describe the passage

This practice will make it easier to find the passage when you want to revisit it in the future.

After you've highlighted the passage, you'll move to the letter E. At this stage you'll *explain* what the text means. By asking some simple questions, with the help of God's Spirit, you can understand the meaning of a passage or verse. Here are a few questions to get you started.

- Why was this text written?
- To whom was it originally written?
- How does this text fit with the verses before and after it?
- Why did the Holy Spirit include this passage in the book?
- What does the Holy Spirit intend to communicate through this text?

At this point you're beginning the process of discovering the specific, personal word God has for you from His Word. What's important is that you're engaging with the text and wrestling with its meaning.

After writing a short summary of what you think the text means, you're ready to move on to the letter A which examines what it means to apply the text. This application is the heart of the process. Everything you've done so far culminates under this heading. As you've done before, answer a series of questions to uncover the significance of these verses to you personally, questions like:

- What does this text teach me about God?
- What does this passage mean today?
- What would the application of this passage look like in my life?
- Does the text identify an action or attitude to avoid or embrace?
- What is God saying to me?

These questions bridge the gap between the ancient world and your world today. They provide a way for God to speak to you from the specific passage or verse. Answer these questions under the A. Challenge yourself to write between two and five sentences about how the text applies to your life.

Finally, below the first three entries, you'll see the letter R for *respond*. Your response to the passage may take on many forms. You may write a call to action. You may describe how you'll be different because of what God has said to you through His Word. You may indicate what you're going to do because of what you've learned. You may respond by writing a prayer to God. For example, you may ask God to help you be more loving or to give you a desire to give more generously. Keep in mind that this is your response to what you've just read.

Notice that all of the words in the HEAR formula are action words: *highlight, explain, apply,* and *respond*. God doesn't want us to sit back and wait for Him to drop truth into our laps. Instead of waiting passively, God wants us to actively pursue Him. Jesus said:

*Keep asking, and it will be given to you. Keep searching, and you will find. Keep knocking, and the door will be opened to you* (Matt. 7:7).

Think of the miracle of the Bible. Over centuries of time, God supernaturally moved in a number of men in an unusual way, leading them to write the exact words of God. He led His people to recognize these divine writings and to distinguish them from everything else that had ever been written. Next God's people brought these sixty-six books together. The preservation and survival of the Bible are as miraculous as its writing. Then God gave men, beginning with Gutenberg's printing press, technological knowledge to copy and transmit the Bible so that all people could have it. All because God has something to say to you.

### MEMORIZING THE WORD

Each week the F-260 OT provides an option for Scripture memory. While many plans for memorizing Scripture are effective, a simple system has been effective for me. All you need is a pack of index cards and a committed desire to memorize God's Word. It's easy. Write the reference of the verse on one side of the card and the text of the verse on the other. Focus on five verses at a time and carry your pack of Scripture cards with you.

Whenever you have a few minutes throughout the day, pull out your pack of Scripture cards and review them. Read the reference first, followed by the verse. Continue to recite the verse until you get a feel for the flow of the passage. When you're comfortable with the text, look only at the reference side of the card to test your recall.

It's important to recite the reference first, then the verse, finishing with the reference again. This will prevent you from becoming a concordance cripple. As a new believer, I was forced to look up every verse in the concordance at the back of my Bible. Sometimes when I quoted a Scripture while witnessing, the person asked me, "Where did you get that?" I could only respond, "Somewhere in the Bible." As you can imagine, that answer isn't effective when sharing with others! By memorizing the references, you'll speak with authority and gain the respect of your hearers when you quote Scripture.

After you master five verses, begin studying five more. Review all of the verses you've learned at least once a week. As your pack grows, you'll be encouraged to keep memorizing Scripture, and you'll experience its powerful effects in your life. For a sample HEAR entry, refer to page 270. For disciple-making resources, check out our website, replicate.org.

WEEK 1

# 1//GENESIS 1

MEMORY VERSE
**Psalm 1:1-2**

OPTIONAL READING
**Psalm 1**

Genesis, the first book in both Christian and Jewish Scripture, starts at the most logical place imaginable: the beginning. In the first chapter, we are going to see some of the most foundational truths about who God is: He is Creator, He is eternal, and He is sovereign over every aspect of creation. More than that, He created mankind with a special privilege: to know, delight in, and walk with Him.

**When you think about creation, what are some things that it tells you about God's character?**

HIGHLIGHT

EXPLAIN

APPLY

RESPOND

# 2//GENESIS 2

**MEMORY VERSE**
**Psalm 1:1-2**

**OPTIONAL READING**
**Psalm 2**

The first chapter showed us an overview of God's creative process. Now, in chapter 2, we are shown a closer look at one of the more personal aspects of creation for everyone reading it: the creation of mankind in His image. Chapter 2 will show us how we were created for community both with each other and with our Creator—a revelation that leaves Adam rejoicing in song!

**What do you think it means to be made in the image of God? What responsibilities come with that?**

HIGHLIGHT

EXPLAIN

APPLY

RESPOND

# 3//GENESIS 3

MEMORY VERSE

**Psalm 1:1-2**

OPTIONAL READING

**Psalm 3**

When God finished creation, He called it very good. But in chapter 3, we are going to see an act of rebellion that caused very good to quickly turn bad. When Adam and Eve disobeyed God's command, they ushered in a series of consequences that the rest of human history has been dealing with ever since. But even when God explained the consequences of their sin, He still spoke whispers of hope about a day when those consequences would be conquered forever.

**Where do you see the tendency to disobey God in your own heart? Take some time to pray and ask God to forgive you and teach you how to obey Him.**

HIGHLIGHT

EXPLAIN

APPLY

RESPOND

MEMORY VERSE

**Psalm 1:1-2**

# 4//GENESIS 4

OPTIONAL READING

**Psalm 4**

When God made Adam and Eve, He gave them a command to "be fruitful, multiply" (Gen. 1:28). Chapter 4 shows us how they followed that command—and how the consequences of their sin began to unfold in their own family. But even in the shadow of deep sadness, this chapter shows us God's faithfulness and mercy.

**When is a time you've been shown mercy? Who is someone you need to show mercy to?**

HIGHLIGHT

EXPLAIN

APPLY

RESPOND

MEMORY VERSE

**Psalm 1:1-2**

OPTIONAL READING

**Psalm 5**

# 5//GENESIS 6

Genesis 6 begins with an aspect of God that we have seen before: His justice. When mankind wreaked havoc on God's perfect creation and actively rebelled against Him, He responded justly. But at the same time, we see an intimate portrait of His mercy—particularly in the way that He spared Noah's family. These two aspects of God are crucial, because they have been present from the beginning, and continue to this day.

**How have you seen the perfect balance of God's justice and mercy at work in your own life?**

HIGHLIGHT

EXPLAIN

APPLY

RESPOND

WEEK 2

# 6//GENESIS 7

MEMORY VERSE
**Psalm 6:1-2**

OPTIONAL READING
**Psalm 6**

At the beginning of Genesis 7, God says that of all the people on earth, Noah alone was righteous (7:1). Noah and his family would board the ark-—along with two of every kind of animal. Though the earth was flooded, God made a way for His people and His creation to continue. As we read about the extent of the flood waters on the earth, we must also be reminded of the incredible mercy God showed by providing Noah—and ultimately all of mankind who would come after him—a means of rescue.

**What do you think it means to live righteously? What do you think it means to live faithfully? In what ways do you see the marks of these two things in your life?**

HIGHLIGHT

EXPLAIN

APPLY

RESPOND

MEMORY VERSE

**Psalm 6:1-2**

OPTIONAL READING

**Psalm 7**

# 7//GENESIS 8

In the aftermath of the flood, God reaffirmed His promise to those He created in His own image. Even though God the Creator would have been perfectly justified wiping the slate entirely clean, He made a promise that we remember to this day: He will never again destroy the earth and its inhabitants with a flood (Gen. 9:11). We are thankful to serve a God who both makes and keeps His promises.

**What is a promise God has made that you need to be reminded of today?**

HIGHLIGHT

EXPLAIN

APPLY

RESPOND

MEMORY VERSE

**Psalm 6:1-2**

# 8//GENESIS 9

OPTIONAL READING

**Psalm 8**

This chapter represents a sort of new beginning—it has a similar command God gave to Adam and Eve, but this time with a twist. God established this command with a covenant; God will never again flood the earth, and mankind is to fill it, care for it, and spread God's image far and wide across it (Gen. 9:1). Remembering God's faithfulness to keep His covenants is crucial, especially as, at the end of the chapter, we begin to see some of the ways humans would prove themselves unfaithful. Even when we are not faithful to the Lord, He is faithful to us.

**How does it feel to know that God is faithful when we are not? Take a moment to pray and thank God for being faithful to you, even when you are not faithful to Him.**

HIGHLIGHT

EXPLAIN

APPLY

RESPOND

MEMORY VERSE

**Psalm 6:1-2**

OPTIONAL READING

**Psalm 9**

# 9//GENESIS 11

In Genesis 5, we read a similar genealogy as we did in chapter 10. It describes the way that humans were beginning to spiral into wickedness—which was then followed by an act of judgment from God. Here we see the same thing, but this time human wickedness was paired with arrogance. They felt they had no need for God, and could make a name for themselves rather than being subject to the One who had named them. But still, even though humanity kept drifting from God and earning His judgment, we get yet another glimpse of hope: a family line from which God's Messiah would come.

**What are ways we try to make a name for ourselves today instead of being who God made us to be?**

## HIGHLIGHT

## EXPLAIN

## APPLY

## RESPOND

# 10//GENESIS 12

**MEMORY VERSE**
**Psalm 6:1-2**

**OPTIONAL READING**
**Psalm 10**

Abram is one of the most crucial figures in Judaism. In the same way Noah enjoyed a special relationship with God even though he was surrounded by wickedness, so too, did Abram. But if humanity was spared from destruction because of God's mercy and Noah's faithfulness, Abram's faithfulness will bring something even more amazing from God: His blessing. Because of the promise God made Abram in Genesis 12, the whole earth would be blessed because of His family—most specifically through the promised Messiah.

**How can you and your family be a blessing on God's behalf to someone today?**

HIGHLIGHT

EXPLAIN

APPLY

RESPOND

WEEK 3

# 11//GENESIS 15

MEMORY VERSE

**Psalm 13:5**

OPTIONAL READING

**Psalm 11**

God promised to make Abram into a great nation, but there was a problem. Abram and his wife were childless. Even though Abram waited, no children came. So God reminded him of the promise that He'd made—and crucially, Abram believed Him. That belief made him be called righteous, or in right-standing with God. Likewise, when we believe in the gospel—the death and resurrection of Jesus for our salvation—God considers us righteous, too.

**Are there ways are you struggling to believe God's promises? What is something you need to believe today?**

HIGHLIGHT

EXPLAIN

APPLY

RESPOND

# 12//GENESIS 16

**MEMORY VERSE**
**Psalm 13:5**

**OPTIONAL READING**
**Psalm 12**

We met her briefly in previous reading, but chapter 16 tells us more about Sarai, Abram's wife. She knew God had promised Abram a son, but she was struggling with unbelief. So she took matters into her own hands and convinced Abram to have a son with her servant, Hagar. This decision led to strife between the two women. But pay close attention to God's faithfulness to Hagar. And she gave Him a name which rings true still to this day (16:13).

**When have you seen your lack of trust in God lead to more problems?**

**What name did Hagar give God? Why is it appropriate?**

HIGHLIGHT

EXPLAIN

APPLY

RESPOND

**MEMORY VERSE**
**Psalm 13:5**

**OPTIONAL READING**
**Psalm 13**

# 13//GENESIS 17

Again, in Genesis 17, God reminds Abram of His promise: He would bless him, He would give him the promised son, Isaac, He would make his descendants as numerous as the stars, and He would receive all of the glory for it. God's faithfulness and ability to do what He says overcomes our flaws, uncertainties, and missteps.

**What do you need to trust God with today?**

## HIGHLIGHT

## EXPLAIN

## APPLY

## RESPOND

# 14//GENESIS 18

**MEMORY VERSE**
**Psalm 13:5**

**OPTIONAL READING**
**Psalm 14**

In light of the covenant formed in Genesis 17, Abram and Sarai now had new covenant names: Abraham and Sarah. And they are about to receive special visitors that Abraham recognizes as the Lord Himself. These visitors bring a mixture of news: Sarah would have a child, and Sodom—where Abraham's relative Lot lived—would be destroyed. But Abraham was about to learn a crucial lesson about the breadth and depth of God's mercy when He revealed that, if only ten righteous people could be found, the entire city would be spared.

**Why do you think Abraham asked God to spare the city if only ten righteous people could be found? Would you have done the same? Why or why not?**

HIGHLIGHT

EXPLAIN

APPLY

RESPOND

MEMORY VERSE

**Psalm 13:5**

# 15//GENESIS 19

OPTIONAL READING

**Psalm 15**

Lot was a righteous man who was grieved by the sin around him, but we meet him at the end of a long period of moral compromise (2 Pet. 2:7-9). He gravitated from looking toward Sodom (13:10), to pitching his tent toward Sodom (13:12), to living in Sodom (14:12), to almost being killed there. And now he was back, sitting in Sodom's gateway. But even though his testimony was all but destroyed from this progression, this one final altercation would prove something we've seen again and again: God is just and abhors wickedness, and God is merciful.

**What would you say is the progression of your life—do you find yourself gravitating closer and closer to sin or taking active steps away from it?**

HIGHLIGHT

EXPLAIN

APPLY

RESPOND

WEEK 4

# 16//GENESIS 20

**MEMORY VERSE**
**Psalm 16:1-2**

**OPTIONAL READING**
**Psalm 16**

If anyone should've trusted God wholeheartedly it was Abraham. But even after God had proven Himself faithful, Abraham still had a hard time trusting that God would care for him. As a result, he lied to the people of Gerar. Still, despite Abraham's sin, God was going to use King Abimelech to show another aspect of His mercy. The same is true for us today—God pours out His mercy for us even when we are unfaithful to Him.

**Are you carrying anything with you—habits, hangups, shame—that makes it hard for you to trust God? If so, what are they and what steps can you take to let them go?**

HIGHLIGHT

EXPLAIN

APPLY

RESPOND

# 17//GENESIS 21

**MEMORY VERSE**
**Psalm 16:1-2**

**OPTIONAL READING**
**Psalm 17**

In Genesis 21, Abraham finally saw the fulfillment of the promise God made to him—that he and his wife would bear a son. When Sarah became pregnant by Abraham and delivered a son exactly as God promised, we are reminded of God's promise-keeping nature. Thankfully, as Abraham's life demonstrates, God is faithful to keep His promises no matter how many times we sin and stumble. God's love outweighs even our biggest weaknesses.

**In what areas are you most likely to struggle with weakness? How can you rely on God to be strong where you are weak?**

HIGHLIGHT

EXPLAIN

APPLY

RESPOND

MEMORY VERSE

**Psalm 16:1-2**

# 18//GENESIS 22

OPTIONAL READING

**Psalm 18**

Genesis 22 contains one of the most famous accounts of Abraham's life: the sacrifice of his son, Isaac. Up until this point, God had seen Abraham through trial after trial, each successive one giving Abraham new opportunities to learn how to trust Him. Now, God puts all of those lessons to the test and steps in to provide the sacrifice He demanded. This reminds us of how God has done the same thing for us—He stepped in and provided a sacrifice on our behalf in the form of His Son, Jesus Christ.

**What is God calling you to trust Him with today?**

HIGHLIGHT

EXPLAIN

APPLY

RESPOND

MEMORY VERSE

**Psalm 16:1-2**

OPTIONAL READING

**Psalm 19**

# 19//GENESIS 24

As Abraham had learned, God is faithful to keep His promises. One of the promises he received was that his offspring would inherit the land of Canaan, which became known as the promised land. In Genesis 24, we see how God, who is all-knowing and all-powerful, continues to work in the lives of His people to accomplish His good purposes.

**Think about a time when you watched God work out His purposes through you. How did this impact your relationship with Him?**

HIGHLIGHT

EXPLAIN

APPLY

RESPOND

MEMORY VERSE

Psalm 16:1-2

# 20//GENESIS 25

OPTIONAL READING

Psalm 20

Abraham died at a "good old age, old and contented" (25:8). In chapter 25, we watch as the narrative transitions from Abraham to his son Isaac—and sets up the next phase in the story God is telling through His people. But as the chapter comes to a close, we begin seeing the rumblings of future conflict. This further demonstrates that God's faithfulness and love of His people has nothing to do with them and has everything to do with His goodness.

**What is one new or forgotten insight you've learned about God as you've read through Abraham's and Isaac's story? What does that insight reveal about God's character?**

HIGHLIGHT

EXPLAIN

APPLY

RESPOND

WEEK 5

# 21//GENESIS 26

MEMORY VERSE

**Genesis 26:3-5**

OPTIONAL READING

**Psalm 21**

Isaac inherited a number of things from his father, Abraham. For instance, he inherited the promise God made Abraham—about the land he was in and numerous descendants. But we also see that he inherited Abraham's tendency to lie when he was fearful, for Isaac told a similar lie as the one Abraham told in Genesis 12. Still, after a rocky start in the land of Canaan, God used the king to reaffirm what He'd told him: "Do not be afraid, for I am with you" (Gen: 26:24).

**In what area of your life do you need to be reminded, "Do not be afraid, for I am with you" today?**

HIGHLIGHT

EXPLAIN

APPLY

RESPOND

# 22//GENESIS 27

**MEMORY VERSE**
**Genesis 26:3-5**

**OPTIONAL READING**
**Psalm 22**

Just as Isaac's life was marked by tension and conflict like his father's—Isaac's sons would continue that trend. Jacob and Esau seemingly came out of the womb at war with each other, divided by selfishness and craftiness. In chapter 27, we see the turmoil between these brothers boil over in a final act of deception. Even though Esau was the firstborn, Jacob tricked him out of his birthright. And now, Jacob tricked him out of his blessing. But he would soon learn that his behavior would have dire consequences.

**Why does God use consequences to teach us lessons?**

HIGHLIGHT

EXPLAIN

APPLY

RESPOND

MEMORY VERSE

**Genesis 26:3-5**

# 23//GENESIS 28

OPTIONAL READING

**Psalm 23**

As Jacob fled to stay with extended family to avoid his brother's wrath, his life began to take a turn. While once he relied on his deception and selfishness, he soon would begin taking steps toward being the faithful patriarch who would lead his family to trust in the Lord. God takes this opportunity to reaffirm the covenant He had made with Jacob's ancestors and promise him, "I am with you and will watch over you wherever you go" (Gen. 28:15). We have this same life-changing promise today.

**Why do you need the reminder, "I am with you and will watch over you wherever you go" today? How should that promise impact the way you think, respond, and act?**

HIGHLIGHT

EXPLAIN

APPLY

RESPOND

# 24//GENESIS 29

MEMORY VERSE

**Genesis 26:3-5**

OPTIONAL READING

**Psalm 24**

The account of Jacob, Laban, Leah, and Rachel is filled with humor, sadness, and a deep irony: the man who gained all he had through deception was about to meet his match—and forfeit fourteen years of his life in the process. The end of the chapter sets up the other half of the problems that have permeated this family's relationships, too: envy. Sin has a way of compounding from generation to generation. But even now, God's hand is still at work; even when we are unfaithful to Him, His faithfulness toward us is unwavering.

**How have you seen sin's tendency to spiral out of control in your own life?**

HIGHLIGHT

EXPLAIN

APPLY

RESPOND

MEMORY VERSE

**Genesis 26:3-5**

# 25//GENESIS 30

OPTIONAL READING

**Psalm 25**

For Leah and Rachel, their respective ability and inability to have children became a source of more jealousy and envy in Jacob's family. As the chapter reveals the circumstances behind the births of each of Jacob's children, though, we are watching something remarkable unfold. As is true of God's providential nature, from these corrupted relationships came twelve sons who eventually became the heads of the twelve tribes of Israel—one of whom would eventually bring forth the Messiah, Jesus Christ, our Redeemer.

**God alone has the power to redeem even our worst character traits. Where do you most need to see God's transforming power in your life?**

## HIGHLIGHT

## EXPLAIN

## APPLY

## RESPOND

## WEEK 6

# 26//GENESIS 31

**MEMORY VERSE**
**Psalm 27:4**

**OPTIONAL READING**
**Psalm 26**

As a result of God's grace and power in his life, Jacob experienced great prosperity during the years when his family was growing. But, this led not to comfort, but to more conflict. In this eventful chapter, Jacob is once again fleeing, but this time because he and his family have been mistreated. Jacob's honesty and assertiveness when confronting Laban show how far he has come from being the deceiving trickster he was when we were first introduced to him.

**How have you seen your own character progress as you've grown? What are some ways you feel you still need to grow so that you can better represent your heavenly Father?**

HIGHLIGHT

EXPLAIN

APPLY

RESPOND

MEMORY VERSE

**Psalm 27:4**

# 27//GENESIS 32

OPTIONAL READING

**Psalm 27**

Genesis 32 represents a pivotal moment in Jacob's life. He had finally parted ways from his father-in-law, but now must prepare to face the person he deceived—his brother, Esau. This chapter highlights the anxiety Jacob felt about the crisis, which led to an unexpected encounter with God. From Jacob's "wrestling match" with God, we are reminded that God will go to great lengths to teach us dependency on Him and the sufficiency of His grace.

**Where do you see the gospel in Jacob's wrestling match with God? How has God shown that gospel and His grace to you in times of resisting or wrestling with Him in the past?**

HIGHLIGHT

EXPLAIN

APPLY

RESPOND

MEMORY VERSE

**Psalm 27:4**

# 28//GENESIS 33

OPTIONAL READING

**Psalm 28**

Genesis 33 shows the power that reconciliation can have on a family. Enough time and life experience had passed between these two brothers that the grudges of their youth were forgotten, and we see Jacob put words to his relief: "I have seen your face, and it is like seeing God's face" (33:10). The face Jacob once fled from now was a welcome sight. God alone could have brought such healing and restoration.

**When have you seen God change someone's heart and behavior? Is there tension in your own relationships that you need to seek the Lord's face and wisdom about?**

HIGHLIGHT

EXPLAIN

APPLY

RESPOND

MEMORY VERSE

**Psalm 27:4**

# 29//GENESIS 35

OPTIONAL READING

**Psalm 29**

After the horrific events of Genesis 34 and Jacob's realization that he and his family needed to renew their commitment to the Lord, Genesis 35 describes how they put away their idols, built an altar to the Lord, and redirected their focus to Him. Scripture is filled with promises from God that still apply to His children today. Regularly strengthening our commitment to God and claiming His promises is a vital part of the life of a Christ-follower.

**Refer to Psalm 16:11, 1 John 1:9, Romans 8:1, and Philippians 1:6. How do these promises affect you today? What are some other promises from God that you can remember?**

**How should these promises shape your perspective, goals, decisions, and actions on a daily basis?**

HIGHLIGHT

EXPLAIN

APPLY

RESPOND

MEMORY VERSE

**Psalm 27:4**

# 30//GENESIS 37

OPTIONAL READING

**Psalm 30**

The narrative now shifts from Jacob to his son Joseph, who is the main character from this point on in Genesis. Being the only son of Jacob's favorite wife, Joseph was Jacob's favorite son—and Jacob didn't keep it a secret. The blatant favoritism caused Joseph's brothers to resent him, and Joseph may have done his part to encourage this rift. But as we see, even though the people God is using are imperfect, God's hand is on the situation, and He can turn even the most wicked of intentions into something that glorifies Him.

**Even if we don't recognize it, God is at work in our trials. How does this truth comfort you today? How does focusing on glorifying God in your trials change the way that you see them?**

HIGHLIGHT

EXPLAIN

APPLY

RESPOND

WEEK 7

# 31//GENESIS 39

MEMORY VERSE

**Psalm 31:3**

OPTIONAL READING

**Psalm 31**

We now find Joseph in Potiphar's house in a position of considerable power—he is Potiphar's right-hand man. But even though he had free reign of Potiphar's house, Joseph never took advantage of that freedom. Joseph didn't sin against God or bring shame to the household—even when he was tempted to do so. And refusing to disobey landed him, once again, in a proverbial pit. But still, despite the unfairness of the situation, Joseph's eyes were cast on the Lord rather than the despair of his situation.

**In what form does temptation most often come into your life? How does the trust Joseph demonstrated in the Lord during this season compare with your own trust in Him?**

HIGHLIGHT

EXPLAIN

APPLY

RESPOND

MEMORY VERSE

**Psalm 31:3**

OPTIONAL READING

**Psalm 32**

# 32//GENESIS 40

To this point, Joseph's ability to interpret dreams had gotten him in nothing but trouble. Now, sitting in prison, Joseph would use his God-given gift for the sole benefit of the cupbearer and baker—with the hope they would remember him later. Joseph's ability to interpret the men's dreams demonstrated how God's presence was active in his life, even if his immediate surroundings didn't make it seem so.

**What is a gift God has given you? How can you use it to build someone else up? How can you use it to glorify God?**

HIGHLIGHT

EXPLAIN

APPLY

RESPOND

MEMORY VERSE

**Psalm 31:3**

# 33//GENESIS 41

OPTIONAL READING

**Psalm 33**

In Genesis 41, God's sovereignty is on full display in several key ways. God prepared Joseph to interpret Pharaoh's dream and positioned him in the exact place to do so. God had set the plan in motion that enabled the Egyptians to survive the coming famine. God orchestrated Joseph's rise in power. Even when others planned evil against Joseph, God used their plans to position Joseph in the perfect place to protect and provide for God's covenant people.

**When you look back over the course of your life, what evidence do you see of God's sovereign control bringing you to where you are today?**

HIGHLIGHT

EXPLAIN

APPLY

RESPOND

MEMORY VERSE

**Psalm 31:3**

# 34//GENESIS 42

OPTIONAL READING

**Psalm 34**

Shifting away from Joseph's narrative now, we begin to see how the famine was affecting those on the outskirts of Egypt. Particularly, we see the way Joseph's family was struggling. Broken and desperate, they sought help from Joseph—even though they didn't recognize him. As Joseph set a plan in motion to bring about reconciliation in his family, we should remember the lengths to which God went to reconcile us to Himself.

**Is there a relationship in your life in need of reconciliation?**

**How can the gospel transform that relationship?**

HIGHLIGHT

EXPLAIN

APPLY

RESPOND

MEMORY VERSE

**Psalm 31:3**

# 35//GENESIS 43

OPTIONAL READING

**Psalm 35**

Without their knowing, Joseph had been testing his brothers to see if their character had changed. The first test—whether or not they would leave their brother Benjamin behind—was designed to reveal their of loyalty to each other. In chapter 43 the testing continues. Joseph needed to know if his brothers had changed during the years they had been apart.

**Have you witnessed someone's character improve over the years? If so, what brought about the change?**

HIGHLIGHT

EXPLAIN

APPLY

RESPOND

WEEK 8

# 36//GENESIS 44

MEMORY VERSE

**Psalm 40:1-3**

OPTIONAL READING

**Psalm 36**

Joseph's final test for his brothers was the most difficult, because it cut to the heart of the evil they intended for him when they sold him into slavery. Joseph was testing Judah's willingness to go in Benjamin's place rather than lose his brother. Joseph needed to know if he was dealing with jealous siblings or men who were willing to sacrifice on behalf of each other.

**Why do you think Joseph wanted to see whether his brothers would choose sacrifice over selfishness?**

HIGHLIGHT

EXPLAIN

APPLY

RESPOND

MEMORY VERSE

**Psalm 40:1-3**

# 37//GENESIS 45

OPTIONAL READING

**Psalm 37**

When Joseph realized his brothers had changed, he couldn't hide his identity any longer. Rather than looking for vengeance or getting his "I told you so" moment, he jumped at the opportunity to reunite with his family. Joseph showed compassion and forgiveness to the brothers who had wronged him. This is a beautiful picture of the forgiveness and compassion God demonstrated for us in Christ. Even though we have sinned against Him, He loves us and made the ultimate sacrifice to draw us back to Himself.

**Have you accepted the forgiveness and compassion God has given you? If so, how has your life changed as a result?**

HIGHLIGHT

EXPLAIN

APPLY

RESPOND

# 38//GENESIS 46

MEMORY VERSE
**Psalm 40:1-3**

OPTIONAL READING
**Psalm 38**

Joseph had suffered mightily during the years he was separated from his family. He didn't realize it at the time, but he was playing a major role in the story God was writing. And after decades apart, Joseph was reunited to his family and he could see that God had worked in ways he could've never imagined. Often times, God uses difficult circumstances to teach us our security is found only in Him.

**How has God used a time of "famine" in your life to bring you closer to Himself?**

HIGHLIGHT

EXPLAIN

APPLY

RESPOND

MEMORY VERSE

**Psalm 40:1-3**

# 39//GENESIS 47

OPTIONAL READING

**Psalm 39**

Pharaoh is an important character in this story: he recognized the Lord's hand on Joseph, he trusted Joseph to make important decisions, and, in the end, this led Egypt—and the surrounding area—to be saved from the famine. Even though Joseph had plenty of opportunity to gloat and tip the scales in his favor, he remained faithful to the leaders God had placed over him, generously putting measures in place that would protect Egypt in the future.

**What does it look like to honor God while at the same time respecting the leaders He has placed ahead of us?**

HIGHLIGHT

EXPLAIN

APPLY

RESPOND

# 40//GENESIS 48

MEMORY VERSE

**Psalm 40:1-3**

OPTIONAL READING

**Psalm 40**

Joseph's story is one that highlights God's faithfulness to His children and His promises. Chapter 48 shows us a picture of what God's family looks like. Even though Joseph's sons were not born in the land of his father, Jacob recognizes them as equals and adopts them into his family—the covenant family that God had promised him. In the same way, Jesus' death and resurrection guaranteed that anyone who believes in Jesus—no matter where they come from or what they've done—becomes an adopted child of God.

**How has being adopted by God into His family changed your identity and purpose in life?**

HIGHLIGHT

EXPLAIN

APPLY

RESPOND

WEEK 9

# 41//GENESIS 49

MEMORY VERSE

**Genesis 50:20**

OPTIONAL READING

**Psalm 41**

One of the things that the Book of Genesis reveals is that God uses imperfect people to work on His behalf and bring about His will on earth. Despite the many ways His people betrayed each other, complicated their relationships with sin, and intended evil toward each other, the book ends with the formation of twelve pillars of God's people: the twelve tribes of Israel.

**What has been the most surprising way God turned "evil" to "good" in the accounts you've read so far? Have you ever seen Him do that in your own life?**

HIGHLIGHT

EXPLAIN

APPLY

RESPOND

# 42//GENESIS 50

**MEMORY VERSE**
**Genesis 50:20**

**OPTIONAL READING**
**Psalm 42**

Fearing for their lives after Jacob's death, Joseph's brothers sought forgiveness from Joseph. In Genesis 50, we see one of Scripture's clearest affirmations of God's sovereignty—the fact that all things are under His control and nothing happens apart from His plan and purpose. When Joseph realized his brothers were fearful of how he might treat them after their father's death he said, "You planned evil against me; God planned it for good to bring about the present result—the survival of many people" (Gen. 50:20). With God's people finally well established, and with Joseph's death and burial, we are going to begin a new chapter, seeing exactly how well they fare in this new beginning.

**When have you had a "new beginning" before? If today is a new beginning for you, what do you need to change in order to follow Joseph's example of faithfulness despite your circumstances?**

HIGHLIGHT

EXPLAIN

APPLY

RESPOND

**MEMORY VERSE**
**Genesis 50:20**

**OPTIONAL READING**
**Psalm 43**

# 43//EXODUS 1

It didn't take long after the miraculous events of Joseph's life for God to put His people's faith in Him to the test. After Joseph died, the Israelites living in Egypt started multiplying and living fruitfully—but soon a new king came to power who wasn't as generous to the Israelites as previous kings had been (Ex. 1:8). He forced all of the Israelites into slavery and then ordered all newborn babies to be killed so that the population wouldn't continue to grow. It seemed hopeless, but once again the stage was set for God to act on behalf of His people in order to bring glory to His name.

**What suffering in your life may God be intending for good?**

HIGHLIGHT

EXPLAIN

APPLY

RESPOND

MEMORY VERSE

**Genesis 50:20**

# 44//EXODUS 2

OPTIONAL READING

**Psalm 44**

Abraham, Isaac, and Jacob were revered by the Israelites because they were the forefathers of their people—the line from which they were descended. But in this chapter, we meet Moses, whom they revered because he grew up to be their deliverer. But his beginnings were fraught with strife. Growing up as a prince in the king's house gave him significant advantages, but seeing the oppression of his people caused him to lash out, killing an Egyptian and sending him on the run. Once again, God is setting the stage to show how He uses broken people to carry out His perfect plans.

**Moses grew up with some significant advantages. What kinds of advantages do you have right now? How can you use those advantages to bring God glory?**

HIGHLIGHT

EXPLAIN

APPLY

RESPOND

MEMORY VERSE

**Psalm 50:20**

# 45//EXODUS 3

OPTIONAL READING

**Psalm 45**

After fleeing to Midian, getting married, and starting a new life as a shepherd, Moses had one of the most famous encounters with God recorded in Scripture. Using a burning bush to attract Moses' attention, God called him to lead the Israelites out of slavery. At that time, God also revealed to Moses His name: Yahweh, "I AM WHO I AM" (Ex. 3:14). One of the great truths about God is that He does not change, a fact tied up in His very identity and name. This helps us know that just as God was faithful in the lives of His Old Testament servants, He continues to prove Himself faithful to us today.

**Take some time to reflect on your own "burning bush" experience—when and how God made Himself known to you—and how He has changed you and used you since then.**

HIGHLIGHT

EXPLAIN

APPLY

RESPOND

WEEK 10

# 46//EXODUS 4

**MEMORY VERSE**
**Psalm 46:1**

**OPTIONAL READING**
**Psalm 46**

God had big plans for Moses, but Moses was not convinced God picked the right man for the job. When he voiced his hesitation at what God had asked of him, God gave him three signs and promised to send his brother Aaron to assist him. Each of the signs—turning the staff into a snake, turning Moses' hand leprous, and turning water into blood—revealed God's power over the created world, which reminded Moses and all the Israelites that God also had the power to set them free. When the two of them teamed up and showed the Israelites God's signs, they worshiped Him, thanking Him for hearing their prayers.

**What kinds of excuses do you find yourself making when you hear God telling you to do something?**

HIGHLIGHT

EXPLAIN

APPLY

RESPOND

MEMORY VERSE

**Psalm 46:1**

# 47//EXODUS 5

OPTIONAL READING

**Psalm 47**

After the worship service at the end of chapter 4, Moses and Aaron made their way to Pharaoh—most likely with the anticipation of a positive outcome. But they soon found out that they might have underestimated the task at hand: even though they did what God told them to do, they were met with a denial of God's existence and heavier oppression for the Israelites they were trying to save. As Moses was about to find out, obedience does not always lead to the easy path. In fact, it is often the opposite—but that doesn't make obedience any less crucial to those who follow Him.

**When is a time you obeyed God even when it was hard? What is something you can do to hear His voice clearer so that you can hear what He is telling you to do?**

HIGHLIGHT

EXPLAIN

APPLY

RESPOND

MEMORY VERSE

**Psalm 46:1**

# 48//EXODUS 6

OPTIONAL READING

**Psalm 48**

When God called Moses, the plan was to use him to set the Israelites free. Yet in the eyes of the Israelites, that plan seemed to backfire. When Moses complained to God, God reminded Moses of His connection to Abraham, Isaac, and Jacob and reaffirmed His covenant with them. He promised once again to deliver the Israelites and bring them into a new land—the promised land. Just like the sufferings of Joseph and Job, God prolonging their suffering had a higher purpose: since Pharaoh would not let the Israelites go, the only way it would happen is through God's power. The same power that they would be able to look back on for generations and remember how marvelously He worked.

**When is a time it has seemed like everything is going wrong in your life? What is a lesson that you took from that?**

HIGHLIGHT

EXPLAIN

APPLY

RESPOND

MEMORY VERSE
**Psalm 46:1**

# 49//EXODUS 7

OPTIONAL READING
**Psalm 49**

Exodus 7 moves into one of the most well-known parts of Moses' story, and one of the most awesome displays of God's power in recorded history. Moses began in Pharaoh's court, performing signs that might have stumped the layman, but were no match for Pharaoh's chief magicians. Slowly, though, the signs that God would perform through Moses would prove that there is one God on the throne, that He is Israel's deliverer, and that He cannot be trifled with.

**Just as God used Moses to make His glory and power known, He uses His people and His church today to do the same. How might God be trying to use you to reveal Him to others?**

HIGHLIGHT

EXPLAIN

APPLY

RESPOND

# 50//EXODUS 8

**MEMORY VERSE**
**Psalm 46:1**

**OPTIONAL READING**
**Psalm 50**

Each time God targeted a specific part of the Egyptian landscape with a plague, He was doing two things. First, it was a direct answer to Pharaoh's challenge of Him. Pharaoh denied God's sovereignty and further oppressed the Israelites, so God was going to do the same thing to all of Egypt. But the second thing He was doing was proving His power over the gods of the land. Each plague directly challenged different gods or goddesses in Egypt. For instance, turning the Nile to blood was a judgment on Apis, Isis, and Khnum, the gods, goddesses, and guardians of the Nile. The plague of frogs was a judgment against Hequet, the frog-headed goddess of birth. Gnats were a judgment on Set, the god of the desert. Flies were a judgment on Uatchit, the fly god. With every stroke, and with each hardening of Pharaoh's heart, God was proving His power and dominion over anything man could conjure.

**What is an area of your life where you need to turn over dominion to the only One who deserves it?**

HIGHLIGHT

EXPLAIN

APPLY

RESPOND

WEEK 11

# 51//EXODUS 9

MEMORY VERSE

**Psalm 51:1-2**

OPTIONAL READING

**Psalm 51**

As God was systematically dismantling Egypt's gods, He was also crippling its economy, which became more apparent with the subsequent plagues. Notably, no livestock that belonged to the Israelites died but the Egyptian livestock was pummeled. Pharaoh had been warned of the distinction but didn't benefit from the information he was given. Despite the evidence, Pharaoh remained obstinate and refused to obey God.

**When is a time you've hardened your heart to God's voice? What is something you can do to ensure your heart is soft and attentive to what God is asking of you?**

HIGHLIGHT

EXPLAIN

APPLY

RESPOND

MEMORY VERSE

**Psalm 51:1-2**

OPTIONAL READING

**Psalm 52**

# 52//EXODUS 10

Whatever crops survived the hail were now attacked by swarms of locusts—yet another judgment on Egypt. The ninth plague, darkness, revealed things were continuing to get worse. You may have also noticed a pattern: Pharaoh initially repents, only to double back on his word and in the process dooms both himself and his people to the plagues God was sending. When we genuinely repent, that repentance will bear fruit: it will be obvious by your actions what has happened in your heart.

**When is a time in your life that you repented and turned back to the Lord? What fruit did that repentance bear in your life?**

HIGHLIGHT

EXPLAIN

APPLY

RESPOND

MEMORY VERSE

**Psalm 51:1-2**

# 53//EXODUS 11

OPTIONAL READING

**Psalm 53**

The purpose of the plagues was that both the Israelites and the Egyptians would recognize the power and glory of God. And this final plague that Moses announced to Pharaoh would be one that was simply impossible to reason away as misfortune or happenstance: God was going to kill every firstborn male in the entire land of Egypt. God was going to leave no justifiable doubt as to who was in control, but He was also going to demonstrate His protection of the Israelites, thus upholding His covenant with Abraham.

**How have you experienced God's grace and protection in your life? How did it confirm to you that God is in control?**

HIGHLIGHT

EXPLAIN

APPLY

RESPOND

MEMORY VERSE

**Psalm 51:1-2**

OPTIONAL READING

**Psalm 54**

# 54//EXODUS 12

On the night of the plague on the firstborn Egyptians, God established Passover—a Jewish holiday that commemorates God's deliverance of the Israelites from Egypt. Passover got its name from the animal blood smeared on the door posts, which marked the Israelites separate from the Egyptians and served as a sign for God's angelic death to "pass over" the house without killing the firstborn. Once the plague came, Pharaoh summoned Moses and ordered the Israelites to leave. With that, the Israelites began their exodus journey. Centuries later, Jesus Christ became the ultimate Passover Lamb when God sent Him to be the sacrifice to save people from the bondage of their sins once and for all. In Jesus, all of the ritual aspects of the Passover described in Exodus 12 find their fulfillment.

**In Christ, God has freed you from slavery to sin and death. Spend time reflecting on your own "exodus" and thank God for His work in your life.**

HIGHLIGHT

EXPLAIN

APPLY

RESPOND

MEMORY VERSE

**Psalm 51:1-2**

# 55//EXODUS 13

OPTIONAL READING

**Psalm 55**

God's presence accompanied the Israelites from the very beginning of their exodus journey, as symbolized by the pillars of cloud and fire that led them on their way. The Israelites had not been out of Egypt long, though, when their fate seemed to take a turn for the worse. Once again God hardened Pharaoh's heart, and Pharaoh gathered an army to track them down and bring them back. Pharaoh's flip-flopping can serve as a reminder to us: is your repentance genuine or is it just a tool you use to get something that you want?

**Where in your life have you seen true repentance? Is there something you need to be done with right now?**

HIGHLIGHT

EXPLAIN

APPLY

RESPOND

WEEK 12

# 56//EXODUS 14

**MEMORY VERSE**
**Psalm 57:2**

**OPTIONAL READING**
**Psalm 56**

Exodus 14 demonstrates that everything the Israelites were experiencing was part of God's plan. Moses encouraged them to trust God, and this encounter culminated in the most famous event in their exodus from Egypt: the parting of the Red Sea. When Moses stretched out his hand, God divided the waters and allowed the Israelites to cross on dry land. But in a final act of judgment against Pharaoh, when his army pursued them, God drove the waters back, drowning them. Finally, the Israelites feared God and believed in Him.

**What truths do you learn about God through the events of the exodus? What impact do these truths have on your faith in God?**

HIGHLIGHT

EXPLAIN

APPLY

RESPOND

# 57//EXODUS 16

When the Israelites complained about their living conditions, God saw to it that every one of their needs were supernaturally met, but with one catch: each day's provisions were only good on the day that they gathered them. This is an important lesson because the same applies to us. Each day is a new opportunity to gather nourishment from God's Word. If we want to remain spiritually fed, we must return to the Scriptures each day for nourishment.

**How consistently are you spending time in the Word? What steps can you can take to make Bible reading a daily practice?**

HIGHLIGHT

EXPLAIN

APPLY

RESPOND

MEMORY VERSE

**Psalm 57:2**

# 58//EXODUS 17

OPTIONAL READING

**Psalm 58**

While the Israelites were learning about God's provision of food and water, God was about to teach them another lesson about His protection. When fighting the Amalekites, the battle took on a peculiar rhythm: When Moses' hands were up, Israel was winning. In verse 12, we see a peculiar word, "steady." This is the first time this word is used in Scripture, and is the same expression used to say "faith" or "faithfulness." Thus, Moses being faithful, or steady, in the raising of his hands demonstrated faith that God would be the One providing victory against Amalek.

**How does the image of Moses raising his hands (and others helping him) give you a bigger picture of what it means to have faith in God?**

HIGHLIGHT

EXPLAIN

APPLY

RESPOND

MEMORY VERSE
**Psalm 57:2**

# 59//EXODUS 19

OPTIONAL READING
**Psalm 59**

After God's miraculous work delivering His people out of Egypt, the Israelites journeyed through the desert, eventually setting up camp at Mount Sinai. On that mountain, God spoke to Moses, telling him that if the Israelites would remember what He had done and obey Him, they would demonstrate that they were His special and holy possession. Our obedience to the Lord is the natural outflow of our joy that comes from realizing that the God of the universe adopts us into His family and makes a way for us to have fellowship with Him.

**What were some of the precautions the Israelites took at Sinai to make sure they didn't defile God's presence? When do you experience God's presence most strongly in your life?**

HIGHLIGHT

EXPLAIN

APPLY

RESPOND

MEMORY VERSE

**Psalm 57:2**

OPTIONAL READING

**Psalm 60**

# 60//EXODUS 20

The Ten Commandments were a set of rules that outlined what holy living looks like—how a consecrated people can know how to live as God's chosen ones. The first four commandments focus on the people's relationship with God, but the next six focus on the people's relationships with each other. The ultimate goal of these commandments isn't to drive the people toward legalistic checklists, but to highlight their need for God and point them toward holiness.

**Have you lived up to God's expectations this week? How does that make you feel about His grace? How does it change your response to it?**

HIGHLIGHT

EXPLAIN

APPLY

RESPOND

WEEK 13

# 61//EXODUS 24

MEMORY VERSE

**Psalm 63:1-3**

OPTIONAL READING

**Psalm 61**

Following some further instructions in chapters 21-23, Exodus 24 shows the Israelites' covenant with God: a promise to obey Him. The ritual sacrifice described in this chapter foreshadows Jesus' death on the cross—an animal's blood was shed as a sacrifice for the sins of the people, which made a way for them to unite with Him.

**How do you think seeing the ritual sacrifice of animals on their behalf made the Israelites feel about their sin? What aspects of this covenant do you also see in Jesus' sacrifice on our behalf?**

HIGHLIGHT

EXPLAIN

APPLY

RESPOND

MEMORY VERSE

Psalm 63:1-3

# 62//EXODUS 25

OPTIONAL READING

Psalm 62

Chapter 25 lays out detailed instructions for specific elements of the tabernacle—the place God was going to dwell in the middle of His people. Each item was intentionally designed to point the worshipers to God, and they were made of a wide range of natural materials, meaning everyone was able to give an offering to help build. Giving is built into our relationship with God as an act of worship.

**Read Exodus 25:22 again. Part of God's instructions included making a way for the people to hear from Him. How can you prepare yourself to hear God speak to you today?**

HIGHLIGHT

EXPLAIN

APPLY

RESPOND

MEMORY VERSE

**Psalm 63:1-3**

# 63//EXODUS 26

OPTIONAL READING

**Psalm 63**

Because of the way God designed the Tabernacle, it could be taken apart and carried as the people continued their journey toward the promised land. It served as a reminder of God's constant presence and their need to center their lives on Him, no matter where they went. The veil of the tabernacle, described in Exodus 26:31-35, separated the ark of the covenant and the mercy seat of God from the rest of the people. In other words, it separated people from the presence of God. When Jesus died, this veil was ripped in half (Luke 23:45), making it apparent that God was now directly accessible for all people.

**Take some time to reflect on what it means to have your own direct access to God. How should it change the way you talk to and about Him?**

HIGHLIGHT

EXPLAIN

APPLY

RESPOND

MEMORY VERSE

**Psalm 63:1-3**

OPTIONAL READING

**Psalm 64**

# 64//EXODUS 27

God's instructions for His house weren't just about the inside; they also applied to the outside. Many of the items that were used to construct God's residence were elements that many modern houses also have. A sink for washing. A grill for burning. Pretty wall coverings and furniture. Burning oil for pleasant aromas and light. God wanted to make it apparent that He was not simply intent on dwelling in heaven, separate from His people; He is a coming-down God who wants to live in the middle of us—even when we are a mess.

**Why is it significant to you that God wants to dwell in our midst, instead of far away and detached? What can you do to draw closer to Him today?**

HIGHLIGHT

EXPLAIN

APPLY

RESPOND

MEMORY VERSE

**Psalm 63:1-3**

# 65//EXODUS 28

OPTIONAL READING

**Psalm 65**

Along with the instructions God gave Moses related to building the tabernacle and its components, He also provided instructions for the creation of the priestly garments—particularly the robes, ephod, and breast-piece worn by the High Priest. This way, the people always knew at a glance whom to approach in order to find the presence of God. But now that we have Jesus as our High Priest, all believers are His priesthood—the people with direct access to God through Jesus' sacrifice. Those around us should be able to see through our actions and attitudes that we are different, set apart for holiness as we bring all people to Him.

**As a member of God's priesthood, is it apparent to those around you that you have permanent access to God's presence? What is a change you can make to make that more apparent?**

HIGHLIGHT

EXPLAIN

APPLY

RESPOND

# WEEK 14

# 66//EXODUS 29

**MEMORY VERSE**
**Psalm 68:5**

**OPTIONAL READING**
**Psalm 66**

After the tabernacle had been constructed and furnished and the priestly garments had been created, everything needed to be dedicated and consecrated for worship. As part of that, God asked the people to give Him their best as an offering, and doing so became a regular part of their obedience to Him. Giving God our best, not what's left, honors Him and shows our gratitude to Him for giving us His best through Christ.

**What does giving God your best look like? What holds you back from offering your best to Him in worship?**

HIGHLIGHT

EXPLAIN

APPLY

RESPOND

MEMORY VERSE

**Psalm 68:5**

# 67//EXODUS 30

OPTIONAL READING

**Psalm 67**

As God wrapped up His instructions for the tabernacle, He described the Day of Atonement—one day a year in which the High Priest made a sacrifice on behalf of the sins of all the Israelites. Before appointing people to head up the building projects, everyone in the camp was to contribute money to complete it. This way everyone had an equal stake in its completion, and would have an equal view of its significance. The writer of Hebrews tells us that the Day of Atonement pointed forward to the sacrifice of Jesus, whose death on the cross cleanses us from our sins once and for all (Heb. 9:24-28).

**We may not sacrifice animals anymore, but the idea of sacrifice is by no means gone from our worship of God. What role do sacrifices still play in your worship of God today?**

HIGHLIGHT

EXPLAIN

APPLY

RESPOND

MEMORY VERSE

**Psalm 68:5**

OPTIONAL READING

**Psalm 68**

# 68//EXODUS 31

God was clear when He emphasized the importance of His people observing the Sabbath. God knows the way that He designed humankind and He knows He designed the human mind, soul, and body with a need for rest. By placing the Sabbath at the beginning of the week, God made His people prioritize resting in Him before beginning their work week. That way, both rest and work are an act of worship.

**What is one way you can prioritize Sabbath rest as a means of worship this week? How could this both honor God and bear witness of your devotion to and trust in Him to others?**

HIGHLIGHT

EXPLAIN

APPLY

RESPOND

MEMORY VERSE
**Psalm 68:5**

# 69//EXODUS 32

OPTIONAL READING
**Psalm 69**

Think for a second about all of the things the Israelites had seen so far. God plagued all of Egypt but spared them. He parted the sea so they could walk through it. He miraculously provided food and water. And still they abandoned Him the first time they had a moment to spare. Like the people Paul condemned in Romans 1, the Israelites preferred to worship created things rather than the Creator Himself. Had Moses not interceded on their behalf, this would have led to their deaths. Our sin, too, warrants death, but Jesus interceded on our behalf, bearing also the wrath that we earned as He hung on the cross.

**What are some created things you have been worshiping in place of the Creator? Confess these in prayer and trust that Jesus is interceding on your behalf even now.**

HIGHLIGHT

EXPLAIN

APPLY

RESPOND

MEMORY VERSE

**Psalm 68:5**

OPTIONAL READING

**Psalm 70**

# 70//EXODUS 33

Despite how angry God was with the Israelites, Moses continued interceding on their behalf—even speaking with God the way that friends speak with each other. But still, Moses was not allowed to view God in His full glory. So God made a compromise: He'd pass by Moses and allow him to see His back. Moses had a unique privilege in his opportunity to communicate with God. Because of Jesus, we too, have the privilege of communicating with our Creator.

**How well do you take advantage of that great privilege?**

HIGHLIGHT

EXPLAIN

APPLY

RESPOND

WEEK 15

# 71//EXODUS 34

MEMORY VERSE

**Psalm 71:5-6**

OPTIONAL READING

**Psalm 71**

Because he was angry at the people's idolatry, Moses smashed the first pair of stone tablets on which God had inscribed His Commandments. But God is merciful and patient, and renewed His covenant with Moses and inscribed a new set of tablets. Additionally, God kept His promise to Moses, allowing him to glimpse His glory, which made his entire face glow—a visible sign that he had met with God. When we spend time with God, He changes us, too—causing others to see His work in our lives through our actions, attitudes, and priorities.

**What are some markers in your life that show you've been meeting with God?**

HIGHLIGHT

EXPLAIN

APPLY

RESPOND

MEMORY VERSE
**Psalm 71:5-6**

# 72//EXODUS 35

OPTIONAL READING
**Psalm 72**

After a brief recap of the commands God had given Moses on the mountain it was time to begin construction of the tabernacle and the elements it contained. The most logical place to start was with the chief craftsmen—people God had gifted with various abilities to carry out the work that was ahead of them. God's people have all kinds of different talents and abilities; using those talents and abilities with excellence is most assuredly an act of worship when they are used to God's glory.

**What is a way God has gifted you? How can you use it for His glory?**

HIGHLIGHT

EXPLAIN

APPLY

RESPOND

MEMORY VERSE

**Psalm 71:5-6**

# 73//EXODUS 40

OPTIONAL READING

**Psalm 73**

The Israelites assembled the tabernacle and all its components just as God instructed. It was a concerted effort on the part of Moses' leadership, the skill of numerous craftsmen, and the gifts of numerous people. After the tabernacle was constructed, Moses consecrated it and appointed Aaron and his sons as priests. Then, God's glory filled the tabernacle, an act showing His approval of their obedience and His presence among them. Additionally, the cloud of God's glory in the temple became the guide for the Israelites' journey. The people had come a long way from their time as slaves in Egypt, despite their repeated sin and disobedience along the way.

**Like the Israelites' journey in the Book of Exodus, God has delivered you from slavery to now walk in His presence every day. Reflect on this truth today and use it as a source of gratitude in your prayers.**

HIGHLIGHT

EXPLAIN

APPLY

RESPOND

MEMORY VERSE

**Psalm 71:5-6**

OPTIONAL READING

**Psalm 74**

# 74//LEVITICUS 8

The tabernacle was a place where God's presence could dwell among His people. For this reason, the people needed to know how to live properly in His presence, which is the purpose of Leviticus and the priesthood it describes. The role of a priest was one of a mediator between God and His people. While Levitical priests served God's purpose well during their time, they are a reminder for us that Jesus is the better priest, as Hebrews 7 describes. These priests sinned, failed, and their time on earth was limited. Moreover, their ability to atone for the people's sins was limited. Our great High Priest, Jesus, is sinless, perfect, and eternal.

**How is your life different because Jesus is sinless, perfect, and eternal?**

HIGHLIGHT

EXPLAIN

APPLY

RESPOND

MEMORY VERSE

**Psalm 71:5-6**

# 75//LEVITICUS 9

OPTIONAL READING

**Psalm 75**

In today's reading, we get a glimpse of some of the elaborate rituals the levitical priesthood would have to go through so that, as verse 6 tells us, "the glory of the LORD may appear to you." These sacrifices and rituals were not the final step of God's plan for His children—instead, they were the precursors, the shadows that come before the real thing. We no longer have to raise and sacrifice animals in order to get the Lord to appear to us, because the perfect sacrifice has already been made on our behalf. God is available right here, right now, and forever—all we have to do is approach Him covered by the blood of the perfect, spotless Lamb.

**How does knowing you have full access and can approach God anytime and anywhere impact your daily relationship with Him?**

HIGHLIGHT

EXPLAIN

APPLY

RESPOND

WEEK 16

# 76//LEVITICUS 16

MEMORY VERSE
**Psalm 77:11-12**

OPTIONAL READING
**Psalm 76**

One of the most important parts of the priest's job was overseeing the Day of Atonement. This day was set aside as the only day of the year when the High Priest could enter the holy of holies and appear before the ark of the covenant. On the Day of Atonement, the High Priest offered sacrifices to seek God's forgiveness for the sins of the people. From the beginning, God has made a way for His sinful people to remain in fellowship with Him, even though they could do nothing to deserve it. The Day of Atonement served this purpose until the crucifixion of Jesus, at which time animal sacrifices for sins were no longer required—thanks to the bodily sacrifice of Jesus Himself.

**What fresh perspective does today's reading give you into your relationship with God?**

HIGHLIGHT

EXPLAIN

APPLY

RESPOND

MEMORY VERSE

**Psalm 77:11-12**

# 77//LEVITICUS 23

OPTIONAL READING

**Psalm 77**

Part of God's plans for His covenant people included several festivals and holidays that served as a time for the people to gather together and worship God. All of the instructions God laid out for His people in Leviticus were intentional, and each of these festivals had important significance for their relationship with God. The Sabbath, which occurred weekly, was a day of rest and reflection meant to refocus the people's attention on God. The festivals celebrated God's redemption of His people from Egypt and His provisions for their physical and spiritual needs. The Day of Atonement constituted a day of self-denial in which the Israelites confessed their sins and the high priest made an atonement sacrifice. These special periods would also help the people remember God's acts of creation, deliverance, protection, and provision.

**Is your worship everything you would like it to be? If not, what steps can you take to incorporate meaningful worship into your daily, weekly, and monthly rhythms of life?**

HIGHLIGHT

EXPLAIN

APPLY

RESPOND

MEMORY VERSE

**Psalm 77:11-12**

# 78//LEVITICUS 26

OPTIONAL READING

**Psalm 78**

God reminded His people not to worship idols and to honor the Sabbath. He declared that obedience to His commands would bring blessing and life, while disobedience would bring curse and difficulty. If, after disobeying, His people repented and sought His forgiveness, they could again experience blessing and life. This cyclical pattern of obedience, blessing, disobedience, cursing, and redemption is the running theme throughout all of the Old Testament, and it's not until Jesus comes that the pattern is finally broken. God's favor is not dependent on our obedience. Because of Jesus' obedience, faith in Him is all that is necessary to have a relationship with God. But it is equally true that if we love God we will obey Him (John 14:15).

**When did God "brake the bars of your yoke" (26:13) and how did that change you?**

**Spend time praising God for His redemption and grace.**

HIGHLIGHT

EXPLAIN

APPLY

RESPOND

MEMORY VERSE
**Psalm 77:11-12**

# 79//NUMBERS 11

OPTIONAL READING
**Psalm 79**

Numbers is the second-to-last book of the Torah, which is the first section of the Hebrew Bible. It picks up with the story of the Israelites' journey from Egypt to the promised land after taking a brief aside in Leviticus to explain the laws that would govern them. After the people built the tabernacle, they resumed their journey to the promised land, but their lack of faith in God again became evident when they complained about their circumstances. The complaining stirred up God's anger, but Moses interceded on behalf of the people, ushering in another miraculous provision of food.

**Do you make it a habit of complaining? If so, what steps can you take to make your concerns a subject of prayer to God rather than complaining to people?**

HIGHLIGHT

EXPLAIN

APPLY

RESPOND

MEMORY VERSE
**Psalm 77:11-12**

# 80//NUMBERS 12

OPTIONAL READING
**Psalm 80**

Moses' relationship with God was special among the people in the camp—something that most, if not all who observed it, noticed. Chief among those who saw and were jealous of his relationship with God were Aaron and Miriam, his brother and sister. When Miriam criticized Moses' marriage and questioned his leadership, God struck her with leprosy, banishing her from the camp for a time. However, Moses again interceded to God for her healing. Both this account and the one in Numbers 11 remind us of our bent toward sinfulness and our need for an intercessor, which we have in Jesus.

**Do you struggle with jealousy? If it's a problem, how might you address it?**

HIGHLIGHT

EXPLAIN

APPLY

RESPOND

WEEK 17

# 81//NUMBERS 13

MEMORY VERSE

**Psalm 84:11**

OPTIONAL READING

**Psalm 81**

Numbers 13 describes sending twelve scouts in to Canaan, the land God promised to Abraham and his offspring. Although God commanded the people to enter the land, ten of the spies returned with a negative report and warned the people not to enter because of the size and strength of the inhabitants. Regardless of whether the report they gave was even true, they were insistent on staying exactly where they were instead of pushing forward in obedience. Only Joshua and Caleb urged the people to overcome their fears and to obey God's command to enter—demonstrating their faith in the promise that God had made them and His ability to see them through safely.

**What is something God has commanded you to do? What excuses have you made to avoid it?**

HIGHLIGHT

EXPLAIN

APPLY

RESPOND

MEMORY VERSE

**Psalm 84:11**

OPTIONAL READING

**Psalm 82**

# 82//NUMBERS 14

Unfortunately, Israel listened to the advice of the ten bringing the negative (and possibly false) report about the land and refused to go forward. As a result, God punished the nation by declaring they would not be the ones to enter the land they were promised. One of God's most evident traits as revealed in the Torah is His justice, which is on display in this tragic scene. Our rebellion against God warrants the same wrath, but thankfully faith in Jesus alone is enough to satisfy God's just anger against our sin. As we grow in faith, we will also grow in obedience and trust in His plan for us, regardless of how daunting the path forward may seem.

**What fears are keeping you from trusting God? Ask God to remove those fears and strengthen your trust in Him.**

HIGHLIGHT

EXPLAIN

APPLY

RESPOND

MEMORY VERSE

**Psalm 84:11**

# 83//NUMBERS 16

OPTIONAL READING

**Psalm 83**

The Israelites would wander in the desert for 40 years, and most would die there, never seeing the promised land. During their wandering years, their rebellion against God grew. Numbers 16–17 describes a rebellion against Moses and Aaron's leadership, led by a Levite named Korah. The rebellion was stopped when God supernaturally destroyed the opponents and sent a plague among the Israelites as divine punishment. God then demonstrated His choice of Aaron and his descendants as priests. One of the most dangerous threats to a person's relationship with God is the illusion of self-sufficiency. Until we surrender complete control to God, we are unable to walk in the freedom and peace He offers.

**In what area of your life do you struggle the most with surrendering control to God?**

**Focus extra prayer and surrender on that area of your life this week.**

HIGHLIGHT

EXPLAIN

APPLY

RESPOND

MEMORY VERSE

**Psalm 84:11**

# 84//NUMBERS 17

OPTIONAL READING

**Psalm 84**

Aaron's rod had a storied history in the Israelites' recent memory. It is the same rod that miraculously became a serpent, turned the waters of the Nile into blood, brought forth plagues from the sea, ground, and the sky, the same rod that was raised to part the Red Sea, and was raised in prayer to defeat the Amalekites. When God caused that staff to bud in the sight of the whole camp, He was reminding them that, although this staff was used in each of those instances, it was God who supplied the power. In the aftermath of squashing Korah's rebellion, God used Israel's memory of this staff to remind them who was in charge.

**When is it easiest for you to forget who is in charge of your life? What comfort does it bring you to turn authority over to the Lord?**

HIGHLIGHT

EXPLAIN

APPLY

RESPOND

MEMORY VERSE
**Psalm 84:11**

# 85//NUMBERS 20

OPTIONAL READING
**Psalm 85**

By this point in Israel's story, forty years had passed since they escaped slavery in Egypt. But just as God stated, most of the people in the camp died in the desert and never stepped foot in the land they were promised because of their disobedience. Unfortunately, this new generation continued with their parents' pattern of rebellion against God for the lack of water at Kadesh. When God told Moses to speak to the rock in order to bring water from it, he decided that he'd rather do things his own way. Acting out of impatience, and perhaps out of hubris, he instead took his staff and struck the rock—disobeying God and claiming credit for giving the people water for himself. This account serves as a tragic reminder that all of us, no matter how holy we appear or how tall our pedestal, are equally susceptible to sin.

**What does this account remind you about God? What warning does it disclose for your relationship with Him?**

HIGHLIGHT

EXPLAIN

APPLY

RESPOND

WEEK 18

# 86//NUMBERS 21

MEMORY VERSE

**Psalm 86:15**

OPTIONAL READING

**Psalm 86**

Yet again, this passage begins with Israel complaining following a miraculous victory. But this account is given a bit of extra weight because it is explicitly referenced by Jesus in John 3 when He is approached by Nicodemus. The scourge of snakes brought on by Israel's rebellious actions is just like the pain of death accompanying mankind's sinful hearts. The only means of salvation is something wholly unfathomable to human minds and only available through God's grace.

**Read John 3:1-18. How does Jesus' commentary on this passage help shed light on the passage? What analogies do you see between this account and what Jesus says in John 3?**

HIGHLIGHT

EXPLAIN

APPLY

RESPOND

MEMORY VERSE

**Psalm 86:15**

OPTIONAL READING

**Psalm 87**

# 87//NUMBERS 22

Balaam's story provides a touch of humor and proof that God works through mysterious means to accomplish His will. Throughout the Torah, we have seen Israel's reluctance to obey (a theme that will continue throughout the entire Old Testament), but this time we are presented with that same theme through a single person's eyes. As you read the account, notice how God goes out of His way to reach the heart of someone who wasn't genuinely seeking Him ... but would certainly find Him in a strange, mysterious way.

**When has God has used an unusual situation to get your attention? What can you do to be more attuned to those circumstances?**

HIGHLIGHT

EXPLAIN

APPLY

RESPOND

MEMORY VERSE

**Psalm 86:15**

# 88//NUMBERS 27

OPTIONAL READING

**Psalm 88**

Moses had faithfully led Israel for decades, but the time had come for Israel to know who would be his successor. The Lord's choice was obvious—one of the faithful spies sent out to Canaan who had been following Moses closely and observing all of the ways he interacted with God. Joshua was commissioned in the sight of all of Israel, which let them know whom to look to after Moses was gone. Joshua exhibited strong leadership characteristics, but most importantly, a servant's heart and an ear bent toward the Lord's will—qualities any of us would be blessed to be able to emulate.

**Do you think that people would be able to say your ear is tuned to the Lord's will? What is a step you can take to walk more closely with Him, starting today?**

HIGHLIGHT

EXPLAIN

APPLY

RESPOND

MEMORY VERSE

**Psalm 86:15**

# 89//NUMBERS 34

OPTIONAL READING

**Psalm 89**

The time for God's people to enter the promised land had come, just as God had promised to Abraham, Isaac, and Jacob. God outlined in great detail how the land would be divided among the twelve tribes of Israel. God intentionally split up the Levites among all of the territories to serve as a reminder of their need for holiness, righteousness, and obedience. God places all kinds of people in our lives to serve as reminders to live holy, righteous, and obedient lives, and it would serve us well to look for them, learn from them, and attempt to emulate them as they follow Christ.

**Who is someone in your life that demonstrates these qualities? What is it like to be around them? How can you adopt some of the things that you've learned from them?**

HIGHLIGHT

EXPLAIN

APPLY

RESPOND

MEMORY VERSE

**Psalm 86:15**

# 90//NUMBERS 35

OPTIONAL READING

**Psalm 90**

In addition to dividing up the Levites among the tribes, God also designated cities of refuge across the land as a place of escape and protection. These cities of refuge were more than just a place of retreat— they were a reminder of God's faithfulness to His people. Even today, God invites all of us, no matter what we have done, to take refuge in Him made possible by Jesus' life, death, and resurrection.

**How would you benefit from the refuge God is offering you today in Christ? What steps can you take to find refuge in Him?**

HIGHLIGHT

EXPLAIN

APPLY

RESPOND

WEEK 19

# 91//DEUTERONOMY 1

MEMORY VERSE
**Deuteronomy 1:29-30**

OPTIONAL READING
**Psalm 91**

The purpose of Deuteronomy is laid out in the first few verses. It is, in large part, the record of Moses' speech to the Israelites as they were about to take up residence in the promised land. It records how God made a covenant with Moses that included the giving of the Law, how they journeyed for forty years in the desert to find it, and that God had specific expectations of His people and how they were to live among outsiders. In the same way, God has expectations of each of us, and He intends for us to live our lives worthy of the gospel we have received (Eph. 4:1).

**Practically speaking, what does it mean for you to live your live worthy of the gospel?**

HIGHLIGHT

EXPLAIN

APPLY

RESPOND

MEMORY VERSE

**Deuteronomy 1:29-30**

# 92//DEUTERONOMY 2

OPTIONAL READING

**Psalm 92**

As Moses began his speech, he reminded the people of what had taken place since leaving Egypt. He reiterated God's faithfulness. He expressed his desire for them to learn from the mistakes of their ancestors. Both Scripture and our relationships with other believers serve a similar purpose in our lives today. As we look back on how God has been faithful to His people throughout history, our own faith and trust in Him is strengthened.

**How is your story one of God's faithfulness? Who could you encourage with it?**

HIGHLIGHT

EXPLAIN

APPLY

RESPOND

MEMORY VERSE

**Deuteronomy 1:29-30**

# 93//DEUTERONOMY 3

OPTIONAL READING

**Psalm 93**

After their arrival at Canaan, Moses reminded the Israelites of the key victories they had seen on the way. For instance, battles that had been fought and won not through sheer strength or numbers, but through the power of God. It is important to look back and take note of the specific ways God has worked on your behalf. Remembering these victories can do wonders in helping us keep our eyes fixed on God even when our circumstances are difficult.

**What is a victory that you've seen in your life that only God could've given you? How can you use that to help someone going through something similar?**

HIGHLIGHT

EXPLAIN

APPLY

RESPOND

MEMORY VERSE

**Deuteronomy 1:29-30**

# 94//DEUTERONOMY 4

OPTIONAL READING

**Psalm 94**

In addition to reminding the Israelites of God's providence over their lives, Moses offered detailed instructions on how they were to live moving forward. What mattered most was that they remain faithful to God through obedience to His commands. Moses warned the people of the temptations idolatry presented. He encouraged them to teach each generation to obey the Lord. Keeping God's laws was essential to the people's prosperity and security. God promised that their wholehearted, consistent obedience would result in long lives in the land. On the other hand, if they disobeyed, they would experience the curses of divine discipline. Even today, we demonstrate our love for God by obeying His ways, teaching younger generations about Him, and declaring the truths of His Word to the world.

**God wanted the people to remember that He alone deserves first place in their lives. What do you find competes with the Lord for your time, attention, or loyalty?**

**What steps will you take to ensure God has first place in your life?**

HIGHLIGHT

EXPLAIN

APPLY

RESPOND

MEMORY VERSE
**Deuteronomy 1:29-30**

# 95//DEUTERONOMY 5

OPTIONAL READING
**Psalm 95**

On the brink of claiming the land they were promised, Moses took a moment to remind the people what kept their society from total chaos—the Ten Commandments. He also recounted the awesome spectacle that announced their arrival. Finally, he reminded the people of the promise they made that day after witnessing the marvel of God's presence on the mountain. Going back to the basics was as important for them as it is for us. Seeing what God asks of us is the first step in acting obediently toward Him, especially on the brink of a new chapter in life.

**When is a time you've gotten a fresh start? How does it help to remind yourself of the basics of obedience to God when beginning something new? What is a fresh start you can make right now?**

HIGHLIGHT

EXPLAIN

APPLY

RESPOND

WEEK 20

MEMORY VERSE

**Deuteronomy 6:4-5**

OPTIONAL READING

**Psalm 96**

# 96//DEUTERONOMY 6

In Deuteronomy 6, we find a foundational command: "Listen, Israel: The LORD our God, the LORD is one. Love the LORD your God with all your heart, with all your soul, and with all your strength" (Deut. 6:4-5). These verses sum up what obedience to God looks like, and it's the command Jesus referenced when He was asked what the greatest commandment was (Matt. 22:37-39).

**Practically speaking, what does it look like to love God above everything else?**

HIGHLIGHT

EXPLAIN

APPLY

RESPOND

MEMORY VERSE

**Deuteronomy 6:4-5**

# 97//DEUTERONOMY 7

OPTIONAL READING

**Psalm 97**

God blesses His people with the intention that we will be a blessing to others. In Deuteronomy 7, God reminded Israel that they had been immeasurably blessed. Today, God's chosen people include all who believe in His Son, and we too, are blessed so we can bless others. Like the ancient Israelites, we are simply recipients of His grace, and He expects the same wholehearted love and obedience from us.

**How can you use the ways you've been blessed to be a blessing to someone else today?**

HIGHLIGHT

EXPLAIN

APPLY

RESPOND

**MEMORY VERSE**
**Deuteronomy 6:4-5**

**OPTIONAL READING**
**Psalm 98**

# 98//DEUTERONOMY 8

Israel had a long history of forgetting how much they relied on God and so Moses warned them of this. In the coming years as they would experience prosperity in the new land, this reminder would prove poignant (and would be made easier by the commands in Deut. 6). Remembering God's great acts of deliverance from the past would be a way to keep their need for Him at the forefront of their minds.

**What helps you remember your dependence upon God? How can you use your dependence on Him to help you grow closer to Him?**

HIGHLIGHT

EXPLAIN

APPLY

RESPOND

MEMORY VERSE

**Deuteronomy 6:4-5**

# 99//DEUTERONOMY 9

OPTIONAL READING

**Psalm 99**

One of the enemies of holiness is self-righteousness. For this reason, Moses reminded the Israelites that they were undeserving recipients of God's grace, pointing to the golden calf episode as a glaring reminder of that truth. God's grace in their lives was based on His righteousness alone, as it is for God's children today. As the apostle Paul points out, "He made the one who did not know sin to be sin for us, so that in him we might become the righteousness of God" (2 Cor. 5:21).

**What is your understanding of God's grace? How does it work? What does it motivate you to do?**

## HIGHLIGHT

## EXPLAIN

## APPLY

## RESPOND

MEMORY VERSE

**Deuteronomy 6:4-5**

# 100//DEUTERONOMY 30

OPTIONAL READING

**Psalm 100**

Despite the Israelites' habitual rebellion, Deuteronomy 30 paints a vivid picture of God's mercy and grace against the rebellious heart of humanity. God promised to remain faithful to His covenant people even though they didn't deserve it. In Deuteronomy 30:11-20, Moses summarized the choice every person faces: the choice of life or death. Moses challenged the people to choose for themselves the path of life and blessing instead of the path of selfishness that leads to death.

**How can you live out Deuteronomy 30:20 today?**

HIGHLIGHT

EXPLAIN

APPLY

RESPOND

WEEK 21

MEMORY VERSE
**Joshua 1:8-9**

OPTIONAL READING
**Psalm 101**

# 101//DEUTERONOMY 31

The time had come for Moses to pass the torch to Joshua. Even for believers who have God's promise of forgiveness and eternal life, walking with Christ involves a continual, conscious choice of walking by faith. Joshua had the chance to be, as the Lord commissioned him to be in verse 6, "strong and courageous." This is not an internal strength that comes from personal bravery, but the strength and courage we get from wholeheartedly leaning in to God.

**What is a situation you are facing right now that requires the strength and courage of the Lord? What does being "strong and courageous" look like for you in this season of life?**

HIGHLIGHT

EXPLAIN

APPLY

RESPOND

MEMORY VERSE
**Joshua 1:8-9**

# 102//DEUTERONOMY 32

OPTIONAL READING
**Psalm 102**

As Deuteronomy comes to a close, we see a song written by Moses recounting God's perfect faithfulness to imperfect people: a song extolling God's righteousness and highlighting man's need for His mercy. Although Moses had disqualified himself from stepping foot in the promised land, God granted him one last mercy. In the final days of his life, God told Moses to ascend Mount Nebo, where he would be able to, at long last, lay eyes on the land God had promised the people he'd led for the last half a century.

**How do you think Moses changed over the course of his life serving the Lord? What are some of the changes that you have seen in your own life?**

HIGHLIGHT

EXPLAIN

APPLY

RESPOND

MEMORY VERSE
**Joshua 1:8-9**

# 103//DEUTERONOMY 34

OPTIONAL READING
**Psalm 103**

Deuteronomy ends with a description of Moses as an unparalleled leader and prophet who had a relationship with God unlike any other person before him. From the time of Moses, God's people looked forward to another Prophet who would come after him. Jesus Christ ultimately fulfilled that expectation. As Hebrews 3 tells us, Jesus is the true Savior who provided a way of redemption from sin, established the new covenant through His death on the cross for our sins, and thus had a greater glory than Moses.

**Think back over the ministry you've seen Moses perform. What are the biggest takeaways that you can apply to your own relationship with God?**

HIGHLIGHT

EXPLAIN

APPLY

RESPOND

# 104//JOSHUA 1

**MEMORY VERSE**
**Joshua 1:8-9**

**OPTIONAL READING**
**Psalm 104**

After Moses' death, God instructed Joshua to prepare the Israelites for entering the promised land. As Joshua faced the greatest challenge of his life, God reassured him about His continuing presence and challenged him to show courage and to carefully follow God's instructions. Undoubtedly, Joshua had his personal doubts: He had a nation who had been wandering in the desert for four decades following his command. He had the weight of more than a million people's opinions weighing on his shoulders. Still, God's command to be strong and courageous echoed in his head as he began preparations to take the land God had promised them.

**What sorts of things do you think Joshua was feeling? Have there been any times you've felt that way? How did you handle those feelings?**

HIGHLIGHT

EXPLAIN

APPLY

RESPOND

MEMORY VERSE

**Joshua 1:8-9**

# 105//JOSHUA 2

OPTIONAL READING

**Psalm 105**

In preparation for entering Canaan, Joshua sent two men to scout the city of Jericho. The men found refuge from Rahab, a prostitute whose house was located on the city wall. Rahab heard about the God of the Israelites and understood He was unique, and that motivated her to action. Before the Israelites entered Canaan, God was making His glory known among the people there. Rahab expressed her faith in God verbally, but even more than that, she acted in ways that demonstrated that her faith was genuine. Hebrews 11:31 points to Rahab as an example of heroic faith.

**In what situations do you need to express faith this week, both verbally and in action?**

## HIGHLIGHT

## EXPLAIN

## APPLY

## RESPOND

WEEK 22

# 106//JOSHUA 3

MEMORY VERSE

**Psalm 107:9**

OPTIONAL READING

**Psalm 106**

Joshua 3 was the moment the Israelites had been waiting for since they escaped Egypt—crossing into the promised land. After a 40-year diversion because of their disobedience, the moment finally came. Just as God miraculously enabled them to cross the Red Sea, He again enabled them to cross the Jordan River on dry land. The two river crossings show God's consistent presence and protection of His people.

**What is something in your life that you have received after a long wait? How did it make you feel?**

HIGHLIGHT

EXPLAIN

APPLY

RESPOND

MEMORY VERSE
**Psalm 107:9**

OPTIONAL READING
**Psalm 107**

# 107//JOSHUA 4

After crossing the Jordan, Joshua instructed one man from each tribe to gather a stone for erecting a memorial. That memorial served as a reminder of God's faithfulness and power for the Israelites and future generations. God continues to work miracles in the lives of His children today, not the least of which is the gift of salvation. Taking time to reflect on God's gifts and miraculous works is a vital part of a relationship with Him.

**What is one way you can incorporate "remembering" into your walk with God this week?**

HIGHLIGHT

EXPLAIN

APPLY

RESPOND

MEMORY VERSE
**Psalm 107:9**

# 108//JOSHUA 5

OPTIONAL READING
**Psalm 108**

The Israelites wandered in the desert for so long that the majority of the generation who crossed the Red Sea were not the same people who crossed the Jordan. This means that their entire lives, all they knew was God's miraculous provision of food in the middle of the sandy stretches all around them. So now, in the land where they would be living, God provided for them in a new way—through the produce of the land that they could cultivate. After a Passover meal and a rededication ceremony to the Lord, they were ready for the next step of their journey—the quest to claim the land God promised.

**How has God provided for you throughout your life? How have you seen His means for provision change?**

HIGHLIGHT

EXPLAIN

APPLY

RESPOND

MEMORY VERSE

**Psalm 107:9**

# 109//JOSHUA 6

OPTIONAL READING

**Psalm 109**

Jericho was the first city to be attacked in their quest to claim the promised land, but before Joshua could formulate a plan, he received a visit from a heavenly messenger who gave him instructions on how to overtake it. Noticeably absent from the plan was any military strategy; Jericho would be overtaken by trust and obedience alone. God was clearly in control of this situation. Joshua needed to display trust in God's plan by following His instructions. On the seventh day, the people marched around the city seven times, blew trumpets, and shouted. Then God intervened miraculously. He delivered the city into the Israelites' hands, all except for Rahab and her family, whom He had promised to protect because she helped God's people. We must always remember that our God keeps His promises. He is who He says He is and does what He says He will do.

**Is there a battle you need God to fight for you today? Choose to trust Him to fight for you, and give Him the room to work without trying to usurp control.**

HIGHLIGHT

EXPLAIN

APPLY

RESPOND

# 110//JOSHUA 7

**MEMORY VERSE**
**Psalm 107:9**

**OPTIONAL READING**
**Psalm 110**

One of the instructions God gave His people as they overtook Jericho was not to seize any wealth or treasures from the Canaanites. God orchestrated this conquest, and the goal was bringing glory to His name, but a focus on material gain would distract the people from this goal. One man, Achan, violated God's instruction, and his greed had a devastating impact on him, his family, and the community as whole. Before the Israelites were going to be able to move on, Joshua would have to confront this sin and handle the collateral damage that comes from directly disobeying the Lord.

**Is there any sin in your life that you need to take before the Lord?**

HIGHLIGHT

EXPLAIN

APPLY

RESPOND

WEEK 23

# 111//JOSHUA 8

MEMORY VERSE
**Joshua 23:14**

OPTIONAL READING
**Psalm 111**

After Achan's sin was brought to light and dealt with, Joshua led the people in a successful conquest of their next city, Ai. Joshua knew this takeover, like Jericho, only happened because God allowed it to, so he responded in worship and a renewal of the covenant with God. The opportunity God gave the Israelites for a second chance to conquer Ai, despite Achan's disobedience, is a reminder of God's grace and willingness to restore those He loves. When we address our sins through confession and repentance, God is quick to forgive us and restore us to a right relationship with Him.

**When have you experienced restoration? Is there restoration in your relationship with God that needs to happen? What about restoration in a relationship with someone close to you? Take a few minutes to take these situations before God in prayer.**

HIGHLIGHT

EXPLAIN

APPLY

RESPOND

MEMORY VERSE
**Joshua 23:14**

OPTIONAL READING
**Psalm 112**

# 112//JOSHUA 23

Chapters 9–22 of Joshua describe the conquering of the promised land and the Israelites' settling in the land. The book ends with Joshua's farewell address to the people, in which he reminded them of God's power and faithfulness to His promises, their need to be strong in faith, obedient to the covenant, and loyal to God. Joshua recapped how God had proven Himself faithful to them and His covenant from as far back as the time of Abraham. Joshua's address closed with a challenge to the people to renew their commitment and worship of God alone, and the people accepted.

**Why is it important for us to constantly renew our commitment to God? How does it make you feel that He never needs to renew His commitment to us?**

HIGHLIGHT

EXPLAIN

APPLY

RESPOND

MEMORY VERSE
**Joshua 23:14**

# 113//JOSHUA 24

OPTIONAL READING
**Psalm 113**

Like the Israelites, we live in a world with influences that might sway us from exclusive devotion to Christ. Joshua's challenge from the previous chapter and the overview of Israel's history from this one reminds us that if we hope to devote our lives exclusively to the Lord, we must hear and obey the Word of God and renew our commitment to Him every day. If we don't, we'll be stuck in the same track the Israelites trod for forty years in the desert—the constant forgetting of what God has done, how far He has brought us, and how far He wants to take us if we'll follow where He leads.

**What changes need to be made in order for you to serve the Lord exclusively? What is the promised reward for doing so?**

HIGHLIGHT

EXPLAIN

APPLY

RESPOND

MEMORY VERSE

**Joshua 23:14**

# 114//JUDGES 2

OPTIONAL READING

**Psalm 114**

Ever since the Israelites left Egypt, they established a dangerous pattern: God would rescue them in spite of their disobedience, they'd stand in awe of the Lord, and then they'd promptly forget everything God had delivered them from. Once Joshua died, God was going to use other means of getting His peoples' attention, dealing with their sin, and constantly bringing them back to Him. Judges 2 serves as an overview of the entire book, but if we're honest, it also looks like the pattern of our lives when we find new and inventive ways to continually shirk our devotion to the Lord as He demonstrates His unfailing faithfulness to draw us back.

**When do you find yourself most prone to wander? What can you do to help keep your eyes fixed on Christ?**

HIGHLIGHT

EXPLAIN

APPLY

RESPOND

MEMORY VERSE

**Joshua 23:14**

# 115//JUDGES 3

OPTIONAL READING

**Psalm 115**

One of the ways God judged the nation of Israel for their unfaithfulness is through allowing many military defeats and oppression by other people groups against them. After this oppression had gone on for several years, the people finally called out to God for mercy. As He had done countless times, God delivered them through Othniel, the first of His appointed judges—the new form of leadership God put in place. This pattern of sin, oppression, repentance, and deliverance through a new judge continues throughout the book, and it paints a clear picture of humanity's bent toward sin and God's inexhaustible love.

**Take a few minutes to reflect on Judges 2–3 and the truths these passages reveal about God. Write down the things you learn about Him from this text and reflect on these truths throughout the day.**

HIGHLIGHT

EXPLAIN

APPLY

RESPOND

WEEK 24

# 116//JUDGES 4

**MEMORY VERSE**
**Psalm 119:18**

**OPTIONAL READING**
**Psalm 116**

When the Israelites turned to evil, God allowed them to be oppressed by a Canaanite king for 20 years, before they finally cried out for deliverance. God heard their cries, and He responded by appointing Deborah as their judge. In addition to being a judge, Deborah was also a prophet who delivered God's messages to the Israelites. She served as God's spiritual spokesperson to Barak, who was Israel's military leader. God used the joint efforts of Deborah and Barak to defeat the Canaanite forces that oppressed His people. Deborah stands out as one of the godly leaders in Israel's history. She listened and obeyed the words of God, had faith in His ability to work through her, and encouraged the ways God was working in other people. Deborah also modeled what Jesus would later confirm—we demonstrate our love for God and obedience to Him through a life of service to others.

**Would someone observing your life from the outside see service as a quality you value? What needs to change in order for you to be a true, good, and faithful servant of Christ, acting out of gratitude for the unearned grace He's lavished on you?**

HIGHLIGHT

EXPLAIN

APPLY

RESPOND

MEMORY VERSE
**Psalm 119:18**

# 117//JUDGES 6

OPTIONAL READING
**Psalm 117**

After the spiritual high and 40 years of peace that came with Deborah's leadership, the Israelites relapsed into idol worship. As a result, God allowed them to suffer oppression for seven years. When the Israelites cried out for help, God called a young farmer named Gideon to deliver them. The first thing revealed about Gideon was his fear, something that would continue to plague him. In fear, Gideon requested two signs of assurance that he truly was speaking with God, which God supplied.

**Have you ever experienced a period of fear which God used to remind you of His presence in your life? How did His presence reassure you in that situation?**

HIGHLIGHT

EXPLAIN

APPLY

RESPOND

MEMORY VERSE

**Psalm 119:18**

# 118//JUDGES 7

OPTIONAL READING

**Psalm 118**

The great test of Gideon's leadership came when God called him into battle against the Midianites, but then reduced the army to just a few hundred men. As God had done in the battle of Jericho, He reminded the people that His presence was all they needed, and they could trust Him to be their Deliverer. We do not need signs from God today to know that He continues to faithfully deliver His people from the oppression of sin. God made His role as Deliverer clear when He sent His own Son to the cross to deliver His people from sin and death.

**What are some things you need to remind yourself are true about God in order to trust Him to be your Deliverer?**

HIGHLIGHT

EXPLAIN

APPLY

RESPOND

MEMORY VERSE

**Psalm 119:18**

# 119//JUDGES 13

OPTIONAL READING

**Psalm 119:1-24**

Another spiritual regression by the Israelites brought another judge onto the scene—Samson. To set Samson apart for God's work, he was bound by the Nazirite vow before his birth, which meant he couldn't cut his hair, touch a corpse or carcass of a dead animal, or consume alcohol. Furthermore, the Spirit of God gave Samson extraordinary strength. Just as God set Samson apart for carrying out His work, as the priesthood of believers, we too, are set apart from the pattern of the world to be beacons proclaiming God's sovereignty and goodness to those around us.

**What do you need to do to set yourself apart as a vessel to be used by God for His purposes?**

HIGHLIGHT

EXPLAIN

APPLY

RESPOND

MEMORY VERSE

**Psalm 119:18**

# 120//JUDGES 14

OPTIONAL READING

**Psalm 119:25-48**

Unfortunately, the gifts that God gave Samson went directly to his head. He was still blessed by God, but, as we will see in the coming chapters, he used those blessings for his own benefit. Here, we see him give in to the passions and lusts of the world by marrying a Philistine woman, something specifically outlawed by God. Early on, we see hints that pride and self-indulgence would be Samson's downfalls. Samson's story reminds us that humility is one of the most important virtues in the kingdom of God. With a healthy, balanced view of ourselves in relation to God, we put ourselves in a position to be used by God and to reflect His humility and love to the world.

**Is there anywhere in your life right now where you might have a false sense of control because of pride? What is one step you can take to overcome that weakness by His strength?**

HIGHLIGHT

EXPLAIN

APPLY

RESPOND

WEEK 25

# 121//JUDGES 15

MEMORY VERSE

**Psalm 119:50**

OPTIONAL READING

**Psalm 119:49-64**

Judges 15 is one of numerous examples that demonstrates God uses broken people to carry out His will. When God gave Samson his supernatural strength, He did so to use him as a tool of protection for Israel. Samson, however, has so far been solely concerned with his own personal gains. Nevertheless, even though Samson used his strength as a tool for his own personal revenge, God still used him to carry out the end result: a thousand dead Philistines. The tragedy of Samson's life is that, while God was going to use him regardless, he would never experience the blessing and abundance of a life lived serving his Creator.

**Why do you think God uses broken people to carry out His will?**

HIGHLIGHT

EXPLAIN

APPLY

RESPOND

**MEMORY VERSE**
**Psalm 119:50**

# 122//JUDGES 16

**OPTIONAL READING**
**Psalm 119:65-88**

Samson fell in love with another Philistine woman—this one named Delilah. Unknown to him, Philistine leaders bribed her to uncover the secret of his strength so that they could capture, humiliate, and kill him. When Delilah shaved off Samson's braids, the Spirit left him and he lost the true source of his strength—God Himself. Samson was then captured and blinded by the Philistines. Still hoping to conquer the Philistines, Samson prayed to the Lord for strength, and his prayer was answered. While God was dishonored by Samson's sinful behavior, God nevertheless honored the calling He had given Samson. God is always faithful to the calling and gifts with which He equips us to serve Him. He responds faithfully to our faith, however weak and confused we may be: "If we are faithless, he remains faithful, for he cannot deny himself" (2 Tim. 2:13).

**How would you rate your present level of faith, specifically related to the calling and gifts God has given you with which to serve Him? Spend time in prayer, asking God to strengthen your faith in Him, repenting of any sins that are distracting you from living out your calling.**

HIGHLIGHT

EXPLAIN

APPLY

RESPOND

MEMORY VERSE

**Psalm 119:50**

# 123//RUTH 1

OPTIONAL READING

**Psalm 119:89-112**

During the time of the judges, a severe famine broke out in Israel, so an Israelite man named Elimelech moved with his wife, Naomi, and two sons from Bethlehem in Judah to the land of Moab. While there, Elimelech died, both sons married Moabite women, and then both sons died. Naomi decided to return to her home in Judah, and Ruth chose to go with her, a choice that revealed her love, her loyalty, and her undying commitment to Naomi. Ruth even went so far as to pledge allegiance to Naomi's God. Ruth's commitment to Naomi speaks volumes about both of these remarkable women—to Ruth's loyalty and to Naomi's character even in the face of tragedy.

**How have you seen people's true character come out during difficult times? What have hard seasons of life revealed about your own character and commitment to the Lord?**

## HIGHLIGHT

## EXPLAIN

## APPLY

## RESPOND

MEMORY VERSE

**Psalm 119:50**

# 124//RUTH 2

OPTIONAL READING

**Psalm 119:113-136**

Once in Bethlehem, Ruth took the initiative to help provide for Naomi by gleaning in the nearby grain fields. In the process, Ruth was noticed and befriended by a man named Boaz, one of Naomi's relatives who provided the two widows with grain and protection in a generous display of kindness. The story of Ruth is the story of God's providential love on display—a love that extends to all people who have faith in Him.

**In what area of your life do you need to trust in God's providence? What is one step you can take this week to help you trust Him more?**

HIGHLIGHT

EXPLAIN

APPLY

RESPOND

MEMORY VERSE

**Psalm 119:50**

# 125//RUTH 3

OPTIONAL READING

**Psalm 119:137-152**

The concept of a family-redeemer is foreign to us today, but was important in Ruth's time. A *goel*, or family-redeemer was someone who took on the responsibility of caring for a woman after her husband died. Without a redeemer, the widow would be left destitute in a society that did not make it easy for widows to prosper. Ruth showed great courage and boldness to ask Boaz to take her in marriage, but Boaz also demonstrated kindness in the way he honored and respected her request. Furthermore, he pointed to a Redeemer who was even grander than he was, someone who could take a terrible situation and turn it around for good: the redeemer who was to come, Jesus Christ.

**Who is someone in your life who needs to see kindness in the face of tragedy? How can you be someone who lives out the gospel in a way that resonates with them today?**

HIGHLIGHT

EXPLAIN

APPLY

RESPOND

WEEK 26

# 126//RUTH 4

MEMORY VERSE

**Psalm 119:156**

OPTIONAL READING

**Psalm 119:153-176**

In response to Ruth's request, Boaz followed the process for becoming her redeemer, and the two eventually married. By giving Ruth a husband and a son, the Lord graciously redeemed Ruth's seemingly hopeless situation. The story of Ruth and Boaz reminds us of the gospel, when Jesus Christ came to earth to be our Redeemer. We were born into the hopelessness of sin, but through the death and resurrection of Jesus, God redeems us, He buys us back into His family, and He secures our eternal future with Him.

**Who do you know who is in need of the redemption Jesus offers? Spend extra time in prayer for that person this week, and seek out an opportunity to share the hope of Christ with him or her by the Spirit's leading.**

HIGHLIGHT

EXPLAIN

APPLY

RESPOND

MEMORY VERSE
**Psalm 119:156**

# 127//1 SAMUEL 1

OPTIONAL READING
**Psalm 120**

During the time of the judges, Israel reached a spiritual low point. The priesthood was corrupt, as the behavior of Eli's sons revealed, and many people turned away from the faith of their forefathers. However, in 1 Samuel, it becomes evident that a remnant of faithful Israelites still remained—including Hannah. She demonstrated selfless obedience and humility before the Lord, setting a precedent that we, today, could stand to learn from.

**What about Hannah's attitude and humility stands out to you? What is something that Hannah models that you can emulate?**

HIGHLIGHT

EXPLAIN

APPLY

RESPOND

MEMORY VERSE

**Psalm 119:156**

# 128//1 SAMUEL 2

OPTIONAL READING

**1 Samuel 2**

After her fervent pleas to the Lord, God grants her the gracious gift of a son. Hannah's obedience to devote Samuel to the Lord's service and her prayer of triumph stands in sharp distinction to Eli's sons, who are wicked and receive God's judgment. In this chapter, we see how harshly God judges Eli's sons' wickedness, but it is tinged with a promise—that He will raise a faithful priest for Himself. This priest is going to be Samuel, the last judge of Israel, who will follow in his faithful mother's footsteps and sacrificially devote his life to the Lord.

**Think about the gifts you give to God. Do they cost you little or are they true sacrifices?**

HIGHLIGHT

EXPLAIN

APPLY

RESPOND

MEMORY VERSE
**Psalm 119:156**

# 129//1 SAMUEL 3

OPTIONAL READING
**Psalm 122**

From the time he was a little boy, Samuel served as an apprentice to Eli, the priest. During this time, God called Samuel to a life of prophetic ministry. While resting near the ark, Samuel heard the Lord speak to him. God took the initiative, as He always does, and after some confusion about whose voice he heard, Samuel submitted to God. Without yet knowing what God was specifically asking, Samuel enlisted himself into service wholeheartedly, demonstrating the kind of faith and trust God looks for in those who serve Him.

**In your own life, what does obedience to God's voice look like? Perhaps you need to make adjustments so you can hear it in the first place. In that case, what adjustments do you need to make so that you can hear and obey?**

HIGHLIGHT

EXPLAIN

APPLY

RESPOND

# 130//1 SAMUEL 8

**MEMORY VERSE**
**Psalm 119:156**

**OPTIONAL READING**
**Psalm 123**

Over the years, Samuel continued to grow in his relationship with God and his responsibilities to the nation during a transitional and unstable time in their history. The people voiced their desire to be more like their neighboring nations, who were all ruled by kings, and they hoped that becoming a monarchy would give them strength against their enemies. So they asked Samuel to appoint a king to govern them—a request that flew in the face of their identity as God's chosen people, set apart from all other nations. God granted their request, but considered it simply another of the many rebellious choices of Israel.

**The people of Israel again failed to trust that God's ways were best. How is God currently at work in your life to lead or change you? What steps do you need to take to acknowledge your trust in Him in that process?**

## HIGHLIGHT

## EXPLAIN

## APPLY

## RESPOND

WEEK 27

# 131//1 SAMUEL 9

MEMORY VERSE
**Psalm 127:1**

OPTIONAL READING
**Psalm 124**

The Israelites rebelled against God by demanding a king, and Samuel, with God's approval, granted their request. Even though a monarchy was not God's desire for the people, God still took it upon Himself to select who would be the nation's first king. God worked through a series of seemingly unrelated events to reveal who that king would be. Saul, in the process of searching for some lost donkeys, solicited the help of Samuel. All of this happened according to God's predicted plan, which revealed to Samuel that Saul was God's appointed leader.

**Israel was consistently demonstrating their lack of obedience and faith in the Lord. What is a sign in your life that you lack obedience and faith?**

HIGHLIGHT

EXPLAIN

APPLY

RESPOND

MEMORY VERSE

**Psalm 127:1**

# 132//1 SAMUEL 10

OPTIONAL READING

**Psalm 125**

From the beginning of Saul's story, we see hints of the life-long struggle that would plague his leadership—a lack of trust in God (9:21; 10:22). God gave the people what they demanded even though they would suffer the consequences of their foolish request. Saul's life is a sad story of unrealized potential, but it's an important reminder of God's desire that we trust Him and His plans for our lives, resulting in our unwavering devotion.

**What is one of the biggest obstacles you face as you aim to trust God with the responsibilities He has given you? What would full surrender require in that area of your life?**

HIGHLIGHT

EXPLAIN

APPLY

RESPOND

# 133//1 SAMUEL 12

**MEMORY VERSE**
**Psalm 127:1**

**OPTIONAL READING**
**Psalm 126**

One of the consequences of Israel's new monarchy was a renewed conflict with the Philistines, Israel's enemy neighbor. Saul experienced military victory, which encouraged the people in their ability to fight back against the Philistines. First Samuel 13 and 14 draw a comparison between the leadership of Saul and Jonathan, Saul's son and commander of half of Israel's army. Saul was consumed by his own selfish goals, to the point that he ignored God's instruction and usurped the role of priest, offering a sacrifice that displeased God. This pattern of disobedience would lead to an abrupt end to Saul's reign, when he would be replaced by David, "a man after [God's] own heart" (13:14, ESV).

**Why do you think God rejected Saul's sacrifice? What warning do you take from that in your own life?**

HIGHLIGHT

EXPLAIN

APPLY

RESPOND

MEMORY VERSE

**Psalm 127:1**

# 134//1 SAMUEL 14

OPTIONAL READING

**Psalm 127**

In contrast to Saul's leadership style, chapter 14 shows us what godly leadership looks like. Godly leadership acknowledges trust in God's power, seeks confirmation from God before acting, and moves forward confidently knowing that God will accomplish His will. This chapter, especially when viewed in conjunction with chapter 13, reminds us that what we believe about God determines the actions we take in daily living.

**Reflect on the attitudes and actions of both Saul and Jonathan. What do you learn about how to approach your relationship with God?**

HIGHLIGHT

EXPLAIN

APPLY

RESPOND

MEMORY VERSE
**Psalm 127:1**

# 135//1 SAMUEL 15

OPTIONAL READING
**Psalm 128**

Saul's repeated disobedience had disastrous consequences for him and his family. God equated Saul's failure to obey with idolatry, and for that, He would remove him as king. Even though Saul's superficial statement of repentance might have seemed genuine, we must remember that the truth we learned about David still applies: God is not concerned with superficial displays of piety—He is interested in our hearts.

**When do you find yourself offering superficial displays of righteousness that do not permeate into your heart? What does genuine repentance look like in your life?**

HIGHLIGHT

EXPLAIN

APPLY

RESPOND

WEEK 28

# 136//1 SAMUEL 16

MEMORY VERSE
**1 Samuel 16:7**

OPTIONAL READING
**Psalm 129**

The stage is set for David, who would go down in history as Israel's greatest king. In 1 Samuel 13:14, Samuel described the next king as a man after God's own heart, but very little else is told about David other than his unassuming build and his work as a shepherd. That didn't matter, though, because God chose him to be king and anointed him with His Holy Spirit, and those were the only qualifications that mattered. The same is true of God's people today—God has chosen you to serve Him, and He has equipped you for that task by giving you the presence of His very Spirit. Like David, the Holy Spirit is committed to making you into a person after God's own heart, and all you have to do is surrender in order to allow Him to do so.

**Take a few minutes to think about the reality of the Holy Spirit's presence and work in your life. What would it look like for you take full advantage of the Holy Spirit's power on a daily basis? What could be the result as you do?**

HIGHLIGHT

EXPLAIN

APPLY

RESPOND

MEMORY VERSE

**1 Samuel 16:7**

# 137//1 SAMUEL 17

OPTIONAL READING

**Psalm 130**

The story of David and Goliath is one of the most well-known encounters in Scripture. The Philistine army challenged the Israelite army to a battle between their greatest champions. The Philistine champion was the giant Goliath, whose presence was so intimidating no Israelite wanted the seemingly impossible challenge of battling him. David (who was simply delivering lunch to his older brothers in the army) was offended by the mockery Goliath hurled against Israel's God, so he used his slingshot and the power of God Himself to defend God's honor and kill the giant.

**How had God used David's life to prepare him for this one moment? What is something small you can be faithful in right now that could be used in the future?**

HIGHLIGHT

EXPLAIN

APPLY

RESPOND

MEMORY VERSE

**1 Samuel 16:7**

# 138//1 SAMUEL 18

OPTIONAL READING

**Psalm 131**

In the aftermath of his victory over Goliath, David's life changed both for the better and for the worse. He discovered a lasting friend in Jonathan and a bitter rival in Saul. David's defeat of the giant Goliath is a great biblical story, but it's more than that—it's also a picture of the gospel. In Christ, we have an even greater King than David—a King who defeated the giants of sin and death in order to set His people free.

**Consider a challenge you're currently facing. How can God be glorified and the gospel be displayed through that situation if you turn to Him for strength?**

HIGHLIGHT

EXPLAIN

APPLY

RESPOND

MEMORY VERSE

1 Samuel 16:7

# 139//1 SAMUEL 19

OPTIONAL READING

Psalm 132

Saul's jealousy of David's accomplishments drove him mad so he ordered David's death. However, Jonathan warned David and he escaped. Once again, Jonathan stands out as a model for believers today. Jonathan understood that God had appointed David to be king, and he knew his father's actions did not bring honor to God. At the same time, seeing Saul's descent serves as a sobering reminder of the hopelessness of our situation apart from Him.

**Do you listen to the promptings of the Spirit as Jonathan and David did, or do you ignore the way as Saul did? How does each response affect us in our walk with the Lord?**

HIGHLIGHT

EXPLAIN

APPLY

RESPOND

MEMORY VERSE

**1 Samuel 16:7**

# 140//1 SAMUEL 20

OPTIONAL READING

**Psalm 133**

Saul was Jonathan's father, but Jonathan was submissive first and foremost to the Lord. Even though David and Jonathan had solidified their friendship with a covenant of loyalty to one another, they were first loyal to their commitment to God. No one had a greater claim on Jonathan's life than God did. As Jesus teaches in the Great Commandment, loyalty and submission to God are to take first priority in the life of a Christian, but this also naturally encompasses loving others, as Jonathan modeled so well.

**Do you truly love God more than anyone and anything else? Keep this question at the forefront of your mind today, and ask God to open your eyes to anything that may be competing with Him for your attention, desire, and focus.**

## HIGHLIGHT

## EXPLAIN

## APPLY

## RESPOND

# WEEK 29

**MEMORY VERSE**
**Psalm 138:2**

**OPTIONAL READING**
**Psalm 134**

# 141//1 SAMUEL 21

Although parts of David's life give a clear foreshadowing of Christ, it doesn't take long for us to be reminded that David was a sinful human being who God chose to use for His glory. David fled into exile because Saul wanted to kill him, and during that time, he made a series of selfish decisions that revealed his lack of faith that God would protect him and bring him into power as He had promised.

**How had David already seen God move in His life and prove that He was worthy of David's trust? What has God done in your life to show that He is worthy of your trust?**

HIGHLIGHT

EXPLAIN

APPLY

RESPOND

MEMORY VERSE

**Psalm 138:2**

# 142//1 SAMUEL 22

OPTIONAL READING

**Psalm 135**

David may not have thought much about his actions, but they had a devastating impact on Ahimelech and 85 other priests who were all murdered by Saul for the role Ahimelech played in assisting David. One of the things that makes David a hero of our faith is his habit of repentance. When David learned of these deaths, he acknowledged his sin and attempted to make it right. Throughout his life, David would sin many times, sometimes with tragic consequences, but he always repented and returned to the Lord. Even more importantly, God always accepted him back and continued to use David to make His name known. Like David, we sin often, but God is quick to forgive us and shower us with His grace when we repent of our sins and return to Him.

**How does it make you feel that God responds to contrition and repentance with forgiveness? What is something you need to repent of right now?**

HIGHLIGHT

EXPLAIN

APPLY

RESPOND

MEMORY VERSE

**Psalm 138:2**

OPTIONAL READING

**Psalm 136**

# 143//1 SAMUEL 23

When David found out that Keilah was under attack from the Philistines, his first action was to ask God what to do. This demonstrates David's growing trust in the Lord and established a precedent for his rule that is different from his predecessor, Saul. Additionally, the chapter closes with another example of David seeking the Lord's help instead of fleeing on impulse. As we grow in our relationship with God, we learn to trust Him more and more as He continues to prove Himself worthy of our faith.

**How have you been able to see your relationship with God grow over this past year? What can you do to ensure that growth continues?**

HIGHLIGHT

EXPLAIN

APPLY

RESPOND

MEMORY VERSE

**Psalm 138:2**

# 144//1 SAMUEL 24

OPTIONAL READING

**Psalm 137**

David wrote Psalm 22 in a time of great despair. Although we don't know the specific situation surrounding that Psalm, the events of 1 Samuel 24 parallel it well. Saul's pursuit of David forced him into hiding in a cave, an isolated place that undoubtedly felt helpless, but when presented with the opportunity to kill Saul, David chose not to. In that moment, David chose to claim God's promises for his life and his future, and to trust God to bring them to fruition. This is the same example Jesus gave us on the cross when He echoed David's cry—"My God, My God, why have you abandoned me?"—but even so, both Jesus and David surrendered their very lives to the plans of their Father.

**Read Psalm 22. How do David's and Jesus' examples encourage you?**

HIGHLIGHT

EXPLAIN

APPLY

RESPOND

**MEMORY VERSE**
**Psalm 138:2**

**OPTIONAL READING**
**Psalm 138**

# 145//1 SAMUEL 25

This chapter chronicles a drama-heavy story with strong personalities, each with their own vices, virtues, and pitfalls. One of the things it highlights is something that would continue to get David into trouble throughout his life—his relationship with women. Though he was a man after God's own heart, David struggled in his personal relationships. In this story, Abigail is portrayed as a kind servant, while David comes across as a warrior with an expanding group of wives. David's motivations notwithstanding, Abigail's kindness and boldness saved many lives and ushered her into a life of royalty.

**What do you think would be considered your greatest weakness? How can you lean on the Lord in that area so that He can use it to glorify Himself?**

## HIGHLIGHT

## EXPLAIN

## APPLY

## RESPOND

# 146//1 SAMUEL 28

**MEMORY VERSE**
**Psalm 141:3**

**OPTIONAL READING**
**Psalm 139**

The final chapters of Saul's story tell of a tragic ending and reveal the consequences of his failure to trust God. After years of failing to listen to God, God finally quit speaking to Saul. When confronted with a new threat from the Philistines, Saul approached a medium—a witch—in hopes that she could speak with Samuel's spirit and get him the spiritual wisdom he needed for this battle. This act was done in direct disobedience to the laws of God—laws Saul had previously sought to uphold by banning the practice of mediums altogether.

**Saul's return to something that he had previously taken a hard stance against is indicative of what a series of small concessions of sin lead to. How have you seen this same downward slide in your own life?**

HIGHLIGHT

EXPLAIN

APPLY

RESPOND

# 147//1 SAMUEL 31

MEMORY VERSE
**Psalm 141:3**

OPTIONAL READING
**Psalm 140**

In chapter 28, Samuel predicted what chapter 31 proved true—the Philistines would defeat the Israelites, and Saul and his sons would die in the battle. What Samuel didn't reveal, though, is that Saul would take his own life. From beginning to end, Saul's life shows us the missed opportunities and spiritual unrest of a person who refuses to live in submission to God.

**What is the biggest takeaway for you from Saul's story and his relationship with God?**

HIGHLIGHT

EXPLAIN

APPLY

RESPOND

# 148//2 SAMUEL 1

**MEMORY VERSE**
**Psalm 141:3**

**OPTIONAL READING**
**Psalm 141**

In 1 Samuel 16, God chose David as the man who would replace Saul as king. After many years of tension, wars, and Saul's downfall, the time for David to take the throne finally arrived. However, this time in David's life was not particularly joyful, because it was marked with grief over the deaths of Saul and Jonathan. David sang a lament to express his sadness, and that same lament became part of the nation's collective grieve for the loss of their king. David's lament marks a transition in the narrative from Saul's life to David's, which remains the focus for the rest of 2 Samuel. When the time of mourning for Saul and Jonathan was over, David asked the Lord to show him what to do next—a question that revealed his reliance upon God and his desire to live out his calling as God's anointed ruler. There was no question that David would be a different king than Saul was and that David was the one whose obedience we should seek to emulate instead.

**In today's reading, what stands out to you about David's relationship with God, and how you can apply those things to your own relationship with Him?**

HIGHLIGHT

EXPLAIN

APPLY

RESPOND

MEMORY VERSE

**Psalm 141:3**

# 149//2 SAMUEL 3

OPTIONAL READING

**Psalm 142**

When we begin serving the Lord, we may have misconceptions about how challenging it will be. As David soon found out, even though Saul is dead, his conflict with those loyal to the former king were far from over. But David demonstrates considerable character and compassion when he learns that a rival general, Abner, is killed as an act of revenge. Instead of rejoicing that one of his enemies is dead, he is furious with the man who killed him. David showed what it looks like to be more concerned with true justice than with personal gain—a mentality perfectly in line with the qualities of someone seeking to love God with their entire being.

**Is it easy or difficult for you to overcome the desire for revenge? How can we show people what God is like by the way we treat those who oppose us?**

HIGHLIGHT

EXPLAIN

APPLY

RESPOND

# 150//2 SAMUEL 5

**MEMORY VERSE**
**Psalm 141:3**

**OPTIONAL READING**
**Psalm 143**

After becoming king, David experienced a number of victories in Canaan, which marked a continuation of God's convenient instructions to take control of the promised land. After these victories and the establishment of his palace in Jerusalem, David realized that the source of His success was the Lord. God had been preparing David through both favorable and difficult circumstances to be the king of Israel, and His providential concern for His people was evident through David's actions. Second Samuel 5:10 notes an important truth that is weaved throughout David's life story: "David became more and more powerful, and the LORD God of Armies was with him."

**If you truly believe that God is with you, what should be notably different about your attitude, actions, and relationship with God?**

HIGHLIGHT

EXPLAIN

APPLY

RESPOND

WEEK 31

# 151//2 SAMUEL 6

MEMORY VERSE
**Psalm 145:8-9**

OPTIONAL READING
**Psalm 144**

As one of his first actions after acquiring Jerusalem and making it his capital, David moved the ark of the covenant to the city. God's laws contained specific instructions for carrying the ark, but the men moving it failed to follow that law, and one man died as a result. The setback caused David to reconsider his plans, and also opened his eyes to the holiness of God. After a three-month delay, he finally completed moving the ark to Jerusalem. Next, David planned a temple to house the ark, but God stopped him. Even though David's motive was good, his desire was not in line with God's purpose or timetable. Construction on the temple would have to wait another generation.

**This event made David aware of God's holiness. When is a time you became aware of God's holiness?**

HIGHLIGHT

EXPLAIN

APPLY

RESPOND

MEMORY VERSE

**Psalm 145:8-9**

# 152//2 SAMUEL 7

OPTIONAL READING

**Psalm 145**

The covenant that God made with David would make any person gasp. It was the promise of a lifetime—not only would God continue the pattern He'd already established of clearing a path before David, but He would build out of David a kingdom that would endure forever. The New Testament writers help us understand that the promises of this covenant with David were ultimately fulfilled in Jesus Christ, our eternal King (Acts 2:22-36).

**What do you learn about God from the covenant He made with David? How does it make you feel that thousands of years later, He brought it to fruition?**

HIGHLIGHT

EXPLAIN

APPLY

RESPOND

# 153//2 SAMUEL 9

**MEMORY VERSE**
**Psalm 145:8-9**

**OPTIONAL READING**
**Psalm 146**

One of the highlights of David's friendship with Jonathan was when Jonathan helped protect David from Saul's wrath. In response to that kindness, David made a promise with Jonathan to always show kindness to Jonathan's descendants. Now, as king, David had the chance to make good on that promise by giving Mephibosheth—Jonathan's crippled son—all of Saul's remaining property, inviting him to live under the protection of the palace.

**What sticks out to you about David and Jonathan's friendship? Do you have a friend like that? Are you a friend like that?**

HIGHLIGHT

EXPLAIN

APPLY

RESPOND

MEMORY VERSE

**Psalm 145:8-9**

# 154//2 SAMUEL 11

OPTIONAL READING

**Psalm 147**

Second Samuel 11 begins the infamous account of David's adultery with Bathsheba, as well as the sinful actions and devastating consequences that followed. While David was God's anointed king who God described as a man after His own heart, he was still a sinful human with temptations and desires. David had an affair with Bathsheba, a woman who was married to a man in David's army. The affair led to a pregnancy, which David attempted to cover up. When the cover-up didn't go as David planned, David had Bathsheba's husband murdered in battle, which highlights the destructive pattern of sin David was trapped in.

**Have you ever found yourself in a destructive pattern of sin? How have you experienced the spiraling nature of sin without repentance?**

HIGHLIGHT

EXPLAIN

APPLY

RESPOND

MEMORY VERSE

**Psalm 145:8-9**

OPTIONAL READING

**Psalm 148**

# 155//2 SAMUEL 12

David tried to keep his sin a secret, but God used the prophet Nathan to expose David's sin and move him toward confession and repentance. This story highlights the devastating consequences of sin in our lives and our relationships, but it also reveals the great lengths God goes to in order to bring us back to Him. Ultimately, this story is a reminder that while David was a great king, Jesus is the true and better King whose sinless, perfect life makes our own victory over sin possible.

**What unconfessed sins in your life does David's story bring to light? Spend time in confession and repentance before God. Then claim the promise you have of victory over sin, which was won for you through Jesus' sacrifice.**

HIGHLIGHT

EXPLAIN

APPLY

RESPOND

WEEK 32

# 156//2 SAMUEL 24

MEMORY VERSE
**Proverbs 3:5-6**

OPTIONAL READING
**Psalm 149**

The last chapter of 2 Samuel continues the theme of God's blessing on David's life and the nation of Israel because of His faithfulness to His covenant. However, the events in this chapter are another example of God temporarily removing His blessing because of sin. The military census David took angered God because it happened at a time when the nation of Israel was at peace, which revealed David's interest in his own power and military success over his trust in the Lord. God responded to David's sin by punishing all of Israel, which opened David's eyes to the error of his ways and led to his confession of sin and repentance. Throughout David's life, we notice a cycle in his relationship with God that makes it look a lot like ours. David moved from a place of worship to sin, then to repentance, then back to worship. Second Samuel ends with David's example of costly sacrifice as a display of his worship toward God.

**David acknowledged that because everything is God's, He deserved sacrifices that cost David everything in response. What is a costly sacrifice you can give to God this week?**

HIGHLIGHT

EXPLAIN

APPLY

RESPOND

MEMORY VERSE

**Proverbs 3:5-6**

# 157//1 KINGS 2

OPTIONAL READING

**Psalm 150**

The Book of 1 Kings picks up where 2 Samuel left off—with the transition from David's kingship to that of his son Solomon. Solomon's rise to power wasn't without controversy—Adonijah, his older brother, saw himself as the rightful heir to the throne, and Solomon killed him in order to maintain peace and establish his authority as king. After David made Solomon king and David was about to die, he gave Solomon some parting wisdom. David told Solomon to make obedience to God his primary ambition so that God would continue to be faithful to His covenant promises. Solomon's predecessors—Saul and David—had learned the hard way the importance of obedience to their covenant with God. Both men had made mistakes that Solomon could learn from, but as his story unfolds, it becomes evident that Solomon too was a broken human leader unable to faithfully uphold his covenant with God. Thankfully, as God's children today, we are recipients of God's covenant of grace, which means our relationship with God is based on Jesus' perfect obedience rather than our own efforts.

**Second Corinthians 5:21 says we are made righteous through the perfect life and sacrificial death of Jesus. Where in your life right now are you most tempted to try and prove yourself as being worthy? How does knowing Jesus has done that for you free you from such a need?**

HIGHLIGHT

EXPLAIN

APPLY

RESPOND

MEMORY VERSE

**Proverbs 3:5-6**

OPTIONAL READING

**Proverbs 1**

# 158//1 KINGS 3

With the kingship secured, Solomon turned his attention to ruling Israel. Early on, God appeared to Solomon in a dream and gave him the opportunity to ask for anything. Solomon knew that the responsibility he had as God's anointed king would require great wisdom, so that is what he asked for. God granted his request and gave him riches and honor as well. The story in 1 Kings 3:16-28 shows God was faithful to give Solomon the wisdom he asked for.

**Have you ever asked God for wisdom? Spend a few minutes in prayer asking God to give you His wisdom, so that you can better discern His will and have the courage to follow it.**

HIGHLIGHT

EXPLAIN

APPLY

RESPOND

MEMORY VERSE

**Proverbs 3:5-6**

# 159//1 KINGS 6

OPTIONAL READING

**Proverbs 2**

During David's time as king, he asked God to let him build a temple for Him, but God told him that was not part of His plan for David's rule. Instead, that became Solomon's primary task as God's anointed leader. In the midst of Solomon's great success and grand projects, God gave guidance on how to genuinely honor Him. The key to honoring the Lord does not lie primarily in outward expressions of devotion, but in learning and obeying His commands. The temple could crumble (and eventually did), but unselfish dedication and service to God bear fruits that last for eternity.

**How does the care shown for building God's house affect the way you view your body, which is a temple for the Holy Spirit?**

HIGHLIGHT

EXPLAIN

APPLY

RESPOND

MEMORY VERSE

**Proverbs 3:5-6**

# 160//1 KINGS 8

OPTIONAL READING

**Proverbs 3**

With the temple and Solomon's own palace complete, Solomon assembled the elders of Israel at Jerusalem. The priests and Levites brought the ark of the Lord and the sacred furnishings from the tabernacle and placed them in the temple. After the Lord's glory in the form of a cloud filled the temple, Solomon offered a prayer of dedication, thanking God for keeping His promise to David, asking God to fulfill the remaining promises He had made to David (2 Sam. 7:5-16), and asking God to hear and answer the Israelites when they prayed in times of need. Then God spoke to Solomon and emphasized the importance of obedience for Israel's continued blessing. The call to obedience surfaces time and again in Scripture, which points to its importance as one of the most important disciplines a follower of God can foster. As Christians today, obedience to God does not earn us salvation—that has been freely given to us through Jesus. Instead, obedience is our loving response to God for who He is and all He has done for us. It's also the primary way we display our devotion to God to a watching world.

**Israel's blessing from God was directly tied to their obedience to Him. Read Ephesians 1:3-14 for a list of some of the spiritual blessings we experience today because of Jesus, and use these blessings as fuel for your obedient love. Pray for eyes to see these blessings as being the true joy set before you, just as Jesus did when He endured the cross.**

HIGHLIGHT

EXPLAIN

APPLY

RESPOND

WEEK 33

# 161//1 KINGS 11

**MEMORY VERSE**
**Proverbs 4:23**

**OPTIONAL READING**
**Proverbs 4**

First Kings 11 marks a turning point for Solomon and the kingdom of Israel. At this point in his life, Solomon had 700 wives and 300 concubines who he allowed to practice pagan religions, even constructing places of worship for them. Solomon's life of excessive wisdom and riches (which were originally gifts from God) led him to compromise his faith and his leadership through disobedience, and the consequences were quick and devastating.

**This is not the first time we've seen God's gifts used as tools of selfish gain instead of worship. What is a gift God has given you that you can use as a way of worshiping Him instead of simply elevating yourself?**

HIGHLIGHT

EXPLAIN

APPLY

RESPOND

MEMORY VERSE

**Proverbs 4:23**

OPTIONAL READING

**Proverbs 5**

# 162//1 KINGS 12

God judged Solomon's unfaithfulness by dividing the kingdom of Israel in two. Tensions had been growing among the tribes, and only the grace of God held the kingdom together. Now that it was no more, the kingdom of God's people divided in two. Although Solomon was a wise and godly ruler for much of his life, the end of his reign is another reminder of our need for a true and better King, which we have in Jesus. We are reminded through this story of God's faithfulness to His people—God did not turn His back on either of the kingdoms, and the story of His faithfulness and pursuit of His people continued on toward completion.

**Spiritual compromise is something against which we must always be on guard. What is one area of weakness that often leads you astray and hurts your relationship with God? Spend time today in prayer, asking for His strength to stand on guard against that temptation.**

HIGHLIGHT

EXPLAIN

APPLY

RESPOND

MEMORY VERSE

**Proverbs 4:23**

# 163//1 KINGS 17

OPTIONAL READING

**Proverbs 6**

After the division of the kingdoms, 1 Kings catalogs a long list of kings of Israel and Judah. The evils of the kings of the divided kingdom gets progressively worse, climaxing with the rule of King Ahab. Verse 31 of chapter 16 tells us that the sins of previous kings were trivial in comparison to the sins of Ahab, which included his blatant worship of Baal, the building of temples and altars to Baal, and his marriage to Jezebel, a priestess of Baal. As great as Ahab's sins were, the worst part was that he committed these sins while leading a nation, which means he inevitably led all of Israel, the chosen people of God, down the same evil path. As chapter 17 documents, it was into this perverse national state that the Lord sent His prophet Elijah to proclaim the truth and judgment of God upon His people in a call for their repentance. Even amid some of Israel's darkest days, the Lord sent a light to His people and offered them a way out of the darkness. He has done the same for us today through the light of the gospel.

**What has God used in your life recently to remind you of His faithfulness to provide what you need for daily strength and sustenance? Have you thanked Him for His provisions? How might thanking Him change your own heart posture and lifestyle in response?**

HIGHLIGHT

EXPLAIN

APPLY

RESPOND

# 164//1 KINGS 18

**MEMORY VERSE**
**Proverbs 4:23**

**OPTIONAL READING**
**Proverbs 7**

First Kings 18 describes one of the highs of Elijah's ministry. God gave Elijah the responsibility to confront the idolatry in the land, so Elijah assembled Ahab and the prophets of Baal on Mount Carmel for a contest between God and Baal. Identical sacrifices were prepared and the deity who would send fire to consume His sacrifice would show Israel whom to worship. The prophets of Baal tried to coax their god to send fire, but nothing happened. After Elijah offered a simple prayer, God responded with fire, causing the people to recognize the power of the One true God.

**What convinces you that God is more powerful than anything else? Does your prayer life reflect this belief? What needs to change for it to do so?**

HIGHLIGHT

EXPLAIN

APPLY

RESPOND

MEMORY VERSE

**Proverbs 4:23**

# 165//1 KINGS 19

OPTIONAL READING

**Proverbs 8**

Elijah's faithfulness on Mount Carmel caused quite a stir, particularly enraging Jezebel, who was now set on killing him. As he fled into the wilderness, he was overcome with the weight of the bounty on his head and the unfaithfulness of the people around him, and he became depressed. The events of 1 Kings 19 demonstrate a side of God that is important for us to remember when we feel as Elijah did—overwhelmed by the weight of the world, alone, and hopeless. It shows us the importance of realizing that God cares for us, He is in control, and that we often look for Him in the grand events when He is actually found in the gentle whispers.

**Have you ever felt like Elijah? What can you change about your life to make more room for listening to that gentle whisper?**

HIGHLIGHT

EXPLAIN

APPLY

RESPOND

WEEK 34

# 166 //1 KINGS 21

**MEMORY VERSE**
**Proverbs 12:11**

**OPTIONAL READING**
**Proverbs 9**

The Book of 1 Kings closes with a picture of the full extent of Ahab's evil and the incomparable grace and mercy of God. Ahab desired the vineyard of a man named Naboth, but Naboth refused to sell it to him. As a result, Jezebel devised a plan to accuse Naboth falsely and have him stoned to death. After Naboth's death, Elijah met Ahab and condemned him. The prophet said that the king's family would come to a disastrous end and that he and Jezebel would die violent deaths. That news led Ahab to do something he had never done before—he repented of his sins and humbled himself before God. With that demonstration of repentance, God postponed the family's destruction until after Ahab's death—an action that shows no one is outside of the reach of God's grace and mercy.

**God showed Ahab grace when he repented of his sins and humbled himself before God. Take some time to write out a prayer of repentance and humility to God, praying through it as you seek Him and listen for His voice.**

HIGHLIGHT

EXPLAIN

APPLY

RESPOND

# 167//1 KINGS 22

**MEMORY VERSE**
**Proverbs 12:11**

**OPTIONAL READING**
**Proverbs 10**

A few years after the events of 1 Kings 21, Ahab encouraged King Jehoshaphat of Judah to join him in a war, but Jehoshaphat insisted on first hearing from God's prophets. While Jephoshaphat was well-intentioned, neither he nor Ahab listened to God's prophet Micaiah, who warned of defeat, and Ahab died in battle. From this story, it is Micaiah who stands out as an example of godly character, despite the love and grace God had shown Ahab. Micaiah's example reminds us that only by being transformed by faith in Christ are we able to understand God's will and receive the strength to stand firm on God's Word in the face of the world's pressures.

**How did Micaiah display godly character? What is something in his character that you can emulate in your own life?**

HIGHLIGHT

EXPLAIN

APPLY

RESPOND

MEMORY VERSE

**Proverbs 12:11**

# 168//2 KINGS 2

OPTIONAL READING

**Proverbs 11**

The Book of 2 Kings picks up the historical narrative of the Northern and Southern Kingdoms where it left off at the end of 1 Kings. In the first five chapters, however, a closer focus on the prophetic ministry appears, especially the transition from Elijah to his successor, Elisha. In chapter 2, we read of Elijah's exit from earth by being taken up to heaven in a chariot of fire. Elisha asked for and received a "double portion" of Elijah's spirit. After Elijah was gone, the biblical writer focused on Elisha as the Lord's prophet. Various events of miraculous healing and signs from the Lord are described in 2 Kings 2–4 as being performed by Elisha among the people. It is interesting to note how so many of Elisha's miraculous works closely parallel those of Jesus in the Gospels—healings, raising from the dead, feeding thousands, and so on. Elisha's miracles helped the people understand that he was God's prophet and that God had not abandoned His people after He took Elijah away. The Gospels provide us with that same assurance today, as we are reminded of the great lengths God went to demonstrate His love for us and to call us to faith in Him. Even after Jesus ascended to heaven, God sent His Holy Spirit who remains our only source of hope and assurance even today.

**What truths about God were you reminded of in today's reading? How is He calling you to respond to those truths?**

HIGHLIGHT

EXPLAIN

APPLY

RESPOND

MEMORY VERSE

**Proverbs 12:11**

# 169//2 KINGS 3

OPTIONAL READING

**Proverbs 12**

Joram's reign over Israel lasted for twelve years. His was a reign marked by wickedness, though not quite the level of wickedness of his predecessors. On one hand, he removed the monument to Baal that his father had made, but on the other hand, he clung to the sins of Jeroboam. His "leadership" in those sins caused Israel to fall into the same patterns. This should cause us to consider both the way that we lead and the way that we follow earthly leaders—people are watching you, whether you know it or not. You are influenced by other people's actions, whether you know it or not. In both cases, it is crucial that we ground our faith in Christ so we don't fall in a pattern of sin.

**Is something you're allowing as a concession an action someone else will take as license to sin? Are you allowing sin in your life only because someone you look up to does them, too?**

HIGHLIGHT

EXPLAIN

APPLY

RESPOND

MEMORY VERSE

**Proverbs 12:11**

OPTIONAL READING

**Proverbs 13**

# 170//2 KINGS 5

Second Kings 5 tells the story of Naaman, an Aramean army commander who came to Israel seeking a cure for his skin disease. The Israelite king sent Naaman to Elisha, who in turn sent instructions for Naaman to wash in the Jordan River. Naaman balked at the idea because he, like many of us today, had too much pride to humble himself before this prophet. It took the persuasion of Naaman's servants to convince him to listen to and trust God's prophet and to follow his instructions. Naaman reminds us that we all are in need of God's healing power because of the way sin wreaks havoc in our lives. As Naaman's example shows, God is ready and willing to cleanse and restore us when we humbly approach Him with our needs.

**What is an area of your life—physical or spiritual—where you need the Lord's healing? What does trusting the Lord with that healing look like for you?**

HIGHLIGHT

EXPLAIN

APPLY

RESPOND

WEEK 35

# 171//2 KINGS 6

MEMORY VERSE
**Proverbs 14:7**

OPTIONAL READING
**Proverbs 14**

When Elisha went to warn the king of Israel about the actions of the king of Aram, it made that king angry—angry enough to send an army to capture him. So the morning Elisha and the small number of men he was with woke up and found themselves surrounded it was alarming. It wasn't until Elisha prayed for them to see the reality of the situation—that they weren't overwhelmed at all—that they understood what it means to be fighting with God at their side.

**When have you felt overwhelmed? In hindsight, was your point of view accurate, or was the reality of the situation different?**

HIGHLIGHT

EXPLAIN

APPLY

RESPOND

# 172//JONAH 1

MEMORY VERSE
**Proverbs 14:7**

OPTIONAL READING
**Proverbs 15**

The "Minor Prophets" is a section of the Old Testament that includes short books by God's prophets who were used exclusively for very specific situations. Jonah was one of these prophets, however reluctant a prophet he was. God tasked him with proclaiming judgment on Nineveh, one of the chief cities in the Assyrian Empire. But his first instinct was to run. In Jonah 1, we see Jonah's reaction, the consequences of his attitude, and God's providence.

**Compare the faith of the sailors with the faith of Jonah, God's prophet. If you had to pick, which of them displayed faith that looks most like yours?**

HIGHLIGHT

EXPLAIN

APPLY

RESPOND

# 173//JONAH 2

**MEMORY VERSE**
**Proverbs 14:7**

**OPTIONAL READING**
**Proverbs 16**

In chapter 1, the sailors were physically saved when God stopped the storm after Jonah's confession. In chapter 2, Jonah was physically saved by God. These physical salvations set the stage for the spiritual salvation through repentance that was at the heart of Jonah's message to the Ninevites. God offers all people today spiritual salvation through the sacrificial work of Jesus who died on the cross to save us from our sins. Then, once we accept God's offer of salvation, we become His messengers, tasked with sharing that good news of the gospel with others.

**Jonah's story shows us that God commands obedience, but He pursues us even when we're disobedient. Have you run from something God has asked you to do? What have you possibly missed out on in doing so? What step do you need to take toward obedience?**

HIGHLIGHT

EXPLAIN

APPLY

RESPOND

MEMORY VERSE

**Proverbs 14:7**

# 174//JONAH 3

OPTIONAL READING

**Proverbs 17**

After the fish spit Jonah out alive, God repeated His command for the prophet to go to Nineveh and deliver a message to its people. This time Jonah did not hesitate to obey. He warned the Ninevites of God's judgment against their sins, and the people responded by believing in God and repenting. Even the king repented and ordered the people to fast, pray, and change their sinful ways.

**Jonah had quite the moment of revelation when he was spared from death, and it moved him to finally carry out what God called him to do. When have you had a moment of clarity like this? What did it motivate you to do?**

HIGHLIGHT

EXPLAIN

APPLY

RESPOND

# 175//JONAH 4

MEMORY VERSE

**Proverbs 14:7**

OPTIONAL READING

**Proverbs 18**

Everyone's heart was changed— except for Jonah's. He was furious that God would spare people known for wickedness—he thought it unfair and was sure God had gotten it wrong. While Jonah waited to see what God would do with the people, God used a shade plant to teach His prophet an important lesson about divine compassion. Jonah's story reminds us how important it is that we have hearts aligned with God's. God has made us His ambassadors to a sinful world, which means we have to open our eyes to the countless people around us who desperately need the grace of God. As we mimic God's compassion, He will increase our heart for the lost and draw us closer to Himself.

**Spend a few minutes making a list of the people in your circles of influence who need to place faith in God's grace. Make these people a focus of your prayers as you brainstorm ways to share the gospel.**

HIGHLIGHT

EXPLAIN

APPLY

RESPOND

# WEEK 36

# 176//HOSEA 1

**MEMORY VERSE**
**Hosea 6:3**

**OPTIONAL READING**
**Proverbs 19**

Hosea was another of God's Old Testament prophets who was given a challenging task in order to communicate God's judgment and mercy to the people of Israel. To paint a symbolic picture, God commanded Hosea to marry a prostitute named Gomer as a representation of Israel's unfaithfulness to God. Hosea did as God told him, and the couple had three children who were each given a name that expressed a divine judgment against Israel.

**How did Hosea's relationship with Gomer represent God's relationship with Israel? How does it represent God's relationship with you?**

HIGHLIGHT

EXPLAIN

APPLY

RESPOND

MEMORY VERSE
**Hosea 6:3**

OPTIONAL READING
**Proverbs 20**

# 177//HOSEA 2

Besides judgment for sin, God also promised restoration—an important reminder of His faithfulness to His people despite their unfaithfulness to Him. Through Hosea, God promised that He would not give up on His people. Just as Hosea continually pursued Gomer despite her unfaithfulness, God does the same for His people even today.

**How does Hosea 2 highlight the incredible gift of forgiveness and restoration of God? How has God shown you forgiveness and restoration?**

## HIGHLIGHT

## EXPLAIN

## APPLY

## RESPOND

MEMORY VERSE

**Hosea 6:3**

# 178//HOSEA 3

OPTIONAL READING

**Proverbs 21**

As a symbol of God's redemptive love for Israel, He ordered Hosea to redeem and restore Gomer. Hosea's redemption of Gomer foreshadowed Jesus' redemption of us. On the cross, Jesus our Bridegroom made a way for us to experience forgiveness and redemption of our sins.

**What does it mean to you to call Jesus your Bridegroom? How does this imagery help you better understand your relationship with Him?**

## HIGHLIGHT

## EXPLAIN

## APPLY

## RESPOND

MEMORY VERSE

**Hosea 6:3**

# 179//AMOS 9

OPTIONAL READING

**Proverbs 22**

Each of God's Old Testament prophets had a specific purpose and focus for their ministry, and for Amos, that calling centered on the rampant idolatry and injustice in the Israelite community. From Amos 1:1, we learn that Amos was not a prophet by trade—he was a sheep breeder. God used Amos to point out how far God's people had strayed from Him. Chapter 9 includes God's message of judgment against the people for their sins, but it also includes His message of hope. God, in His justice, had to punish the people for their sins, but He also promised that after the time of judgment, He would restore and repair the broken nation out of faithfulness to His covenant promises. God promised that "David's fallen shelter" (9:11) would be restored—a promise that was ultimately fulfilled in Jesus, the Messiah, who descended from David's earthly line and brought about the justice and redemption the people needed desperately.

**How does your reading in Amos challenge you to act differently as you represent Christ in your community?**

HIGHLIGHT

EXPLAIN

APPLY

RESPOND

# 180//JOEL 1

MEMORY VERSE
**Hosea 6:3**

OPTIONAL READING
**Proverbs 23**

Although each of God's prophets had their own unique calling, a common theme runs throughout all of these books of the Old Testament: God judges sin and calls His people to repentance. This theme surfaces again in the Book of Joel. During Joel's day, a severe locust plague overtook Judah, an event that Joel understood to be a sign of God's looming judgment against the people for their lack of concern and conviction over sin. One of the problems the people faced was their assumption that because they were descendants of Abraham, they would be safe from God's judgment, regardless of their behavior. But God, in order to remain righteous and just, could not ignore their sin, so out of compassion for His people, He sent the plague as well as the prophecy of a coming invasion to draw them back to Himself.

**A common theme throughout the Old Testament is God sending a plague for the specific purpose of drawing people back to Himself. How have you seen trouble in your own life draw you closer to God?**

HIGHLIGHT

EXPLAIN

APPLY

RESPOND

WEEK 37

# 181//JOEL 2

MEMORY VERSE

**Isaiah 9:6**

OPTIONAL READING

**Proverbs 24**

We see God's mercy on display when He promised to restore anyone who repents of sin. God also promised His Holy Spirit who would serve as a sign of His mercy and relationship with them. The apostle Peter quoted Joel 2:28-32 during his Pentecost sermon to assure the people that God was faithful to fulfill the promise He had made (Acts 2:16-21). God has an endless supply of mercy, which He is overjoyed to shower on you when you turn back to Him, regardless of how far you've wandered.

**What do you think it means that God is just? What do you think it means that He is merciful? How do you see both of these qualities in this book—and in your own life?**

HIGHLIGHT

EXPLAIN

APPLY

RESPOND

MEMORY VERSE

**Isaiah 9:6**

# 182//JOEL 3

OPTIONAL READING

**Proverbs 25**

The Book of Joel ends with a reminder of God's power and justice, two of His attributes that are constantly at work in our lives. Additionally, He does all things in the lives of humanity for a single purpose: that we will know He is God and we are not (Joel 3:17). When we reflect on these traits, we are reminded of the grace God has shown us and should be brought to awe that He has chosen sinful humans like us to be His beloved children.

**What is one way you can remind yourself of God's mercy and justice throughout the coming week? How should it affect the way you respond to everyday situations and events?**

HIGHLIGHT

EXPLAIN

APPLY

RESPOND

# 183//ISAIAH 6

MEMORY VERSE
**Isaiah 9:6**

OPTIONAL READING
**Proverbs 26**

The Book of Isaiah demonstrates God's holiness and grace and issues a call for His people to return to Him in obedience and faith. Isaiah 6 records Isaiah's encounter with God when he was called to be a prophet. Isaiah's response to God's commission—"Here I am! Send me."—is one of the greatest pictures of obedience in all of Scripture.

**Re-read the description of God's throne room. What feelings does that inspire in you? When are you most in awe of God's holiness?**

HIGHLIGHT

EXPLAIN

APPLY

RESPOND

MEMORY VERSE

**Isaiah 9:6**

OPTIONAL READING

**Proverbs 27**

# 184//ISAIAH 9

In Isaiah 9, we read the first of many Messianic prophecies in the book when God promised the birth of a child who would deliver His people. Matthew revealed in his Gospel that Isaiah's prophecy pointed to the birth of Jesus, the One who takes away the sins of the world. Despite our disobedience and sinfulness, God has given us a Redeemer in Jesus, and through Him, we gain eternal life in the presence of that same glorious God Isaiah witnessed.

**Read Isaiah 9:6-7 again and reflect on the titles of Jesus in that passage. What do these titles teach you about Him and how He is at work in your life? What is He calling you to do or become in response?**

HIGHLIGHT

EXPLAIN

APPLY

RESPOND

MEMORY VERSE

**Isaiah 9:6**

OPTIONAL READING

**Proverbs 28**

# 185//ISAIAH 44

While the first half of Isaiah is about God's judgment for people's sins, the second half brings words of peace and hope to the people as He reminds them of His covenant by continuing to point them to the coming Messiah. In today's reading, God reminded the people that He chose them, and that He alone—not any of their manmade idols—has the power to restore them. With powerful imagery, God listed numerous ways that the people's idols were foolish and helpless to save them.

**Look back at all of the statements God makes about Himself in this chapter. Which of them stands out to you the most? How does it affect the way you see Him?**

HIGHLIGHT

EXPLAIN

APPLY

RESPOND

WEEK 38

# 186//ISAIAH 45

MEMORY VERSE

**Isaiah 53:6**

OPTIONAL READING

**Proverbs 29**

At the end of Isaiah 44, Isaiah prophesied about how King Cyrus of Persia would defeat the Babylonians and help bring God's people back from exile. Now, in chapter 45, he reminds us that God alone is the Creator and Sustainer of the world and that He orchestrates everything according to His will and good purposes. When life seems hopeless and God seems far away, God's faithfulness to His people throughout Scripture reminds us that He is always at work in our lives.

**Spend time in prayer today reflecting on God as your Creator and Sustainer and praising Him for His work in and through you. Pray also that He would enable you to honor Him in all you say and do in response.**

HIGHLIGHT

EXPLAIN

APPLY

RESPOND

MEMORY VERSE
**Isaiah 53:6**

# 187//ISAIAH 52

OPTIONAL READING
**Proverbs 30**

This chapter and the next are part of Isaiah's "Servant Song": a lengthy prophecy about a Suffering Servant that God would send one day to redeem His people. The end of this chapter, in particular, begins a perfect description of what Jesus, the coming Suffering Servant, would endure—and how He would be exalted. Each of the Gospels in their accounts of Jesus' crucifixion demonstrate how Isaiah's description was spot-on, even though it was written almost a thousand years before the events would take place.

**Isaiah's prophecies are only some of the hundreds of prophecies that Jesus fulfilled. How does it make you feel that you can follow the One all of Scripture points to? What can you do to walk closer with Him today?**

HIGHLIGHT

EXPLAIN

APPLY

RESPOND

MEMORY VERSE
**Isaiah 53:6**

# 188//ISAIAH 53

OPTIONAL READING
**Proverbs 31**

Unlike the Israelites, who continued to fall into patterns of disobedience and lack of faith, the coming Servant would be obedient and faithful always, even at the cost of His own life. As people living on this side of the cross, we know that only Jesus, the Son of God, could live the perfect and sinless life necessary to be the sacrifice for our sins. When we reflect on the suffering Jesus endured and the lengths God went to in order to offer us forgiveness and eternal life in Him, we can't help but want to live our lives in service to Him.

**How do you need to respond today to Jesus' voluntary suffering on your behalf?**

HIGHLIGHT

EXPLAIN

APPLY

RESPOND

MEMORY VERSE

**Isaiah 53:6**

OPTIONAL READING

**Job 1**

# 189//ISAIAH 65

Through God's use of Isaiah, the Israelites were convicted of their sins, recognized God's faithful love, and prayed for Him to again look with favor upon them (Isa. 63–64). The book closes with God's response to Israel's prayer, which was a final reminder of His faithful love and their repeated disobedience. God used Isaiah to tell the people that they would be punished for their sins but that they would also be restored to Him, and eventually, that restoration would be eternal.

**Isaiah was only one of the prophets who was sent to convict Israel about their sin—and to tell of the hope that comes from repentance. When is a time you've been convicted of your sin? How can you set up a support system today that will help point out sin in your life when you don't see it?**

HIGHLIGHT

EXPLAIN

APPLY

RESPOND

MEMORY VERSE

**Isaiah 53:6**

# 190//ISAIAH 66

OPTIONAL READING

**Job 2**

As a result of Israel's response to God's correction, people everywhere would recognize God for who He is and serve and worship Him in response. This is yet another example of God redeeming His people, but not only for their sake—most importantly, for people all around them. From the vision of the future in Revelation, we are reminded that one day this eternal worship will be a reality for all of God's people, regardless of where they are, what they've done, or when they live. And so, in the meantime, we are to serve God and live for Him today.

**What truths about God has your reading of Isaiah revealed to you?**

## HIGHLIGHT

## EXPLAIN

## APPLY

## RESPOND

WEEK 39

# 191//MICAH 1

MEMORY VERSE

**Micah 1:3-4**

OPTIONAL READING

**Job 3**

The prophet Micah's ministry overlapped with Isaiah's and shared many of the same themes, but Micah targeted his prophecies at the southern kingdom, Judah. Like Isaiah, Micah's prophecies describe God's judgment of wickedness and His mercy for those who come to Him in repentance and faith. The main sin God spoke out against was idolatry. These were God's people, but they rejected Him and His laws by allowing and even participating in idol worship. As we saw in Isaiah, though, Micah also prophesied about the hope that would come through a Deliverer.

**What does idolatry look like today? Where do you see it popping up in your life? What can you do to combat it?**

HIGHLIGHT

EXPLAIN

APPLY

RESPOND

MEMORY VERSE

**Micah 1:3-4**

OPTIONAL READING

**Job 4**

# 192//MICAH 5

Micah, like Isaiah, announces what is coming in Israel's future regarding the promised Deliverer of all of humanity. In this chapter, he proclaims a few different messianic prophecies about Jesus, including His birth in Bethlehem, His second coming, and eternal reign. Some of these promises have already come to pass. However, we can have confidence in God, knowing that He will be faithful to do all He has promised. The promised return of Jesus gives us the hope and strength we need to face all of life's present difficulties, and it should motivate us to live in daily obedience to Him.

**How can you apply what you have read this week to a particular situation you are dealing with? How might God be glorified in you as you do?**

HIGHLIGHT

EXPLAIN

APPLY

RESPOND

MEMORY VERSE
**Micah 1:3-4**

# 193//2 KINGS 17

OPTIONAL READING
**Job 5**

In Genesis, God made a covenant with Abraham that He reiterated to Isaac and Jacob, and that promise included plans for a specific portion of land where God's people would live. However, today's reading in 2 Kings reveals that, because of the people's cyclical pattern of disobedience, they lost inheritance of the promised land. Through countless judges, prophets, and other leaders, God repeatedly warned the people to turn back to Him, but they abandoned His invitation, causing God to allow them to be taken captive by the Assyrians and forced into another exile.

**Why are verses 40-41 so frustrating to read? Could someone write similar statements about your life? If that's true, what needs to change?**

HIGHLIGHT

EXPLAIN

APPLY

RESPOND

MEMORY VERSE

**Micah 1:3-4**

# 194//2 KINGS 18

OPTIONAL READING

**Job 6**

Around the same time that the Israelites were going to be forced into another exile, King Hezekiah attempted to reform the Southern Kingdom of Judah by leading the people back to God. Chapters 17 and 18 remind us that God's judgment is serious, but it is never without just cause. God had shown His people incredible grace, but they refused to turn to Him. Furthermore, Hezekiah is a reminder for us that no matter how tempted or pressured we may feel to turn our backs on God, we can always trust in His goodness and sovereignty over our lives.

**What are some of the things in your life you are more tempted to trust in than God? Confess those idols to God and ask Him for the strength and faith to trust in Him alone.**

HIGHLIGHT

EXPLAIN

APPLY

RESPOND

MEMORY VERSE

**Micah 1:3-4**

# 195// 2 KINGS 19

OPTIONAL READING

**Job 7**

King Hezekiah was a man of God, as evidenced through his prayers. Hezekiah prayed to God for deliverance from Assyria, and God delivered the city. He was a wise king who was careful to seek godly counsel and respond in ways consistent with one seeking God's will, and God rewarded that diligence by answering Hezekiah's prayers through His prophet Isaiah, and then miraculously delivering his armies from the camp of the Assyrians.

**Do you have godly counsel in your life? Do you seek them out regularly? If neither of these are true, what is something you can do today to move in that direction?**

HIGHLIGHT

EXPLAIN

APPLY

RESPOND

WEEK 40

# 196//1 KINGS 20

MEMORY VERSE

**Jeremiah 1:4-5**

OPTIONAL READING

**Job 8**

Later, when Hezekiah was suffering from a terminal illness, he prayed for God to remember his faithfulness, and God added 15 more years to his life. However, Hezekiah wasn't perfect, and when he acted prideful over his treasures (which were blessings from God that Hezekiah took for granted), the prophet Isaiah warned him that eventually Judah would experience a fate like Israel's, and all his treasures would be gone.

**Why is it very tempting for us to focus so hard on our earthly treasures? Why is it so dangerous? Where do you find yourself doing the same thing Hezekiah did?**

HIGHLIGHT

EXPLAIN

APPLY

RESPOND

MEMORY VERSE

**Jeremiah 1:4-5**

# 197//2 KINGS 21

OPTIONAL READING

**Job 9**

After Hezekiah died, the nation was ruled by two of its most wicked kings to date. God warned that His judgment was pending, but the kings, particularly Manasseh, did nothing to correct the errors of their ways. While God's grace and patience for His people is limitless, we all come to a place where we must face the consequences of our sins. In those moments, it is crucial to remember that God never withholds his love and grace from us. We are the ones who have drifted from Him.

**What evidence have you seen of God's patience with you recently, and how do you need to respond? How can you demonstrate that same patience to others?**

HIGHLIGHT

EXPLAIN

APPLY

RESPOND

MEMORY VERSE

**Jeremiah 1:4-5**

OPTIONAL READING

**Job 10**

# 198//2 KINGS 22

King Josiah stood in sharp contrast to his father Amon and his grandfather Manasseh, and as a result, significant cultural changes began to take place during Josiah's reign. While God's temple was being repaired, the Book of the Law—Genesis to Deuteronomy—was discovered, and upon hearing it read, Josiah realized the nation was guilty of breaking the covenant and in danger of divine wrath. God's Word has always had the power to bring sin to light and turn hardened hearts toward repentance.

**How have you felt your heart softening to the ways of the Lord as you've filled your heart with His Word?**

HIGHLIGHT

EXPLAIN

APPLY

RESPOND

MEMORY VERSE

**Jeremiah 1:4-5**

# 199//2 KINGS 23

OPTIONAL READING

**Job 11**

Josiah renewed the covenant before the people and initiated a spiritual reform movement that rid the nation of idolatry and renewed times of worship and celebration before God. While these were all positive changes, Josiah was the last righteous king of Judah. His death paved the way for the judgment against sin that God's prophets had warned against. Josiah's example reminds us that our obedience to God is rooted in our relationship with Him and our acceptance of the authority of His Word in our lives.

**Does the Word of God have the ultimate place of authority and priority in your life?**

**What makes the Word more worthy of authority and priority than all other things?**

HIGHLIGHT

EXPLAIN

APPLY

RESPOND

# 200//JEREMIAH 1

**MEMORY VERSE**
**Jeremiah 1:4-5**

**OPTIONAL READING**
**Job 12**

Jeremiah became God's prophet during the reign of King Josiah and remained a prophet through the last of Judah's kings. This was a tumultuous time in the nation's history, and God had stern warnings He wanted His people to hear through His prophet. It's no surprise that Jeremiah was hesitant to obey God's calling. Jeremiah tried to avoid God's call with various excuses, but God revealed to the prophet that He had chosen him before birth for this very task. Idolatry—a violation of the first and second commandments—was revealed as the sin the people were guilty of, which in turn created a rift in their relationship with God. Through Jeremiah, God offered the people another chance for repentance, but He also warned of the judgment that was coming. Like Jeremiah, our task as God's representatives today is to listen to His Word, obey His call, and share the truth of His love and the need for repentance with others.

**What excuses have you used lately to avoid serving God in a particular way? How does Jeremiah's encounter with God speak into that situation?**

HIGHLIGHT

EXPLAIN

APPLY

RESPOND

WEEK 41

# 201//JEREMIAH 25

MEMORY VERSE
**Jeremiah 29:13**

OPTIONAL READING
**Job 13**

For 23 years, Jeremiah delivered the same call of repentance to the people of Judah, but they refused to listen to him. Unfortunately, the time for God's judgment had come, and Jeremiah told them that the nation was about to be overpowered by the Babylonians. Jeremiah described a cup of God's wrath that all the wicked nations would drink as punishment from God, imagery that brings to mind Jesus' prayer in the garden of Gethsemane prior to His crucifixion: "My Father, if it is possible, let this cup pass from me. Yet not as I will, but as you will" (Matt. 26:39). By going to the cross, Jesus drank the cup of God's wrath, taking all sin of humankind on Himself in order to satisfy God's divine justice.

**How does Jesus' action at the cross enable you to have hope in the Lord?**

HIGHLIGHT

EXPLAIN

APPLY

RESPOND

MEMORY VERSE

**Jeremiah 29:13**

# 202//JEREMIAH 29

OPTIONAL READING

**Job 14**

In Jeremiah 29, we read that God used the prophet to provide hope to some of the people of Judah who had been taken into exile in Babylon. Jeremiah sent a letter to them, encouraging them to make the best of their situation because the exile would last for seventy years. Jeremiah warned the exiles not to listen to false promises and to fix their hope on God. In the same way, modern-day believers need to fix their ultimate hope in Christ.

**What is something you've put your hope into that has ultimately let you down?**

HIGHLIGHT

EXPLAIN

APPLY

RESPOND

# 203//JEREMIAH 32

MEMORY VERSE

Jeremiah 29:13

OPTIONAL READING

Job 15

The beginning of the Book of Jeremiah contains prophecies about God's judgment against the people of Judah for their sins, but as Jeremiah's prophecies continue, the predictions shift to promises of God's restoration and hope. Because God's love for the people was unending, He planned to establish a new covenant with His people—one based on the transformation of their hearts rather than on laws engraved on stone tablets. The Lord would be with His people, and they would truly know Him.

**How is the establishment of a new covenant—one written on our hearts instead of stone tablets—good news for you today?**

HIGHLIGHT

EXPLAIN

APPLY

RESPOND

MEMORY VERSE

**Jeremiah 29:13**

OPTIONAL READING

**Job 16**

# 204//JEREMIAH 33

In conjunction with Jeremiah 32, this chapter records various promises the Lord made concerning His restored people. He would give them a blessed and hopeful future. Nothing would be too difficult for the Lord to accomplish on their behalf. He would establish an unbreakable covenant with them in the future. God's promised new covenant is a reality for all Christians today, and it is based on the sacrificial blood of Jesus who made a way for us to have our own personal relationships with God and the indwelling presence of the Holy Spirit in our lives.

**Are you ever tempted to be frustrated over the things you want but feel God hasn't granted you? How can you remind yourself of the fullness of what He's already given you in His new covenant?**

HIGHLIGHT

EXPLAIN

APPLY

RESPOND

# 205//JEREMIAH 52

**MEMORY VERSE**
**Jeremiah 29:13**

**OPTIONAL READING**
**Job 17**

The final chapter of Jeremiah predicts the fall of Jerusalem as God sent forth His judgment on the people. Here, we read a narrative of those events, which will also be chronicled in 2 Kings 24-25. But more than just prophesying events to come, this chapter also serves as a vindication of Jeremiah's entire ministry. His entire work as a prophet was fraught with difficulty and hardship, but in the end, he did as he was told to do by the Lord—and the events to come proved that every single word of it was true.

**Why is it reassuring to you that God follows through on the things He promises?**

HIGHLIGHT

EXPLAIN

APPLY

RESPOND

WEEK 42

# 206//2 KINGS 24

MEMORY VERSE
**Ezekiel 36:26-27**

OPTIONAL READING
**Job 18**

Just as Jeremiah 52 predicted, Jerusalem fell in accordance with God's judgment on the people. Second Kings 24 tells how, three months after Jehoiachin became king, the king of Babylon (Nebuchadnezzar) invaded Judah, took captive the king and his family as well as thousands of leading citizens, and installed Zedekiah, Jehoiachin's relative, as a puppet ruler. These were the beginnings of the events foretold in Jeremiah 52, and set the stage for the period of Israel's history called the Babylonian Exile.

**How has unfaithfulness to God led to unforeseen hardship in your life? How can you strengthen your faithfulness to Him even in difficult times?**

HIGHLIGHT

EXPLAIN

APPLY

RESPOND

MEMORY VERSE

**Ezekiel 36:26-27**

OPTIONAL READING

**Job 19**

# 207//2 KINGS 25

Thirty-seven years after being taken captive to Babylon, King Jehoiachin received a pardon from Evil-merodach, the new Babylonian ruler. Jehoiachin's life improved, although he remained a king-in-exile for the rest of his life. Jehoiachin's release signaled the hope of restoration for Judah. God finally held the people of Judah accountable for their centuries of sin and rebellion against Him, but unlike His unfaithful people, God proved even in judgment that He was still faithful, and that in Him, we find restoration and hope.

**What evidence have you seen of God's faithfulness? How does God's faithfulness bring you hope?**

HIGHLIGHT

EXPLAIN

APPLY

RESPOND

# 208//EZEKIEL 36

MEMORY VERSE

**Ezekiel 36:26-27**

OPTIONAL READING

**Job 20**

With the fall of Jerusalem, the people of Judah were exiled to Babylon. The prophet Ezekiel delivered God's messages to His people while they were in exile, and he was an exile himself. At the heart of Ezekiel's prophecy is God's deliverance and restoration of His people (Ezek. 36:24-26). That God preserved a remnant of exiles from the Northern and Southern Kingdoms reminds us that He never allowed His people to be completely destroyed. Even though the ultimate consequence of sin is death, God kept a remnant for His glory and the good of the world.

**The remnant that God kept served as a beacon of hope to the world. How can you be a similar beacon to the world around you?**

HIGHLIGHT

EXPLAIN

APPLY

RESPOND

MEMORY VERSE

**Ezekiel 36:26-27**

OPTIONAL READING

**Job 21**

# 209//EZEKIEL 37

This restoration was the imagery behind Ezekiel's vision of the valley of dry bones in chapter 37. Instead of decomposition, God composes. Instead of decay, God restores. Through the power and truth of the Word of God and the presence of the Holy Spirit, you and I are becoming more alive each day, much like the dry bones. When we become Christians, God raises us from spiritual death. As our old nature is dying, our new nature is growing, and God is putting His words in our mouths so we can offer a message of hope and life within a world of death and decay.

**If the message that brings life from death is the message of the gospel, who is one person in your sphere of influence who needs to hear this message?**

HIGHLIGHT

EXPLAIN

APPLY

RESPOND

MEMORY VERSE

**Ezekiel 36:26-27**

# 210//DANIEL 1

OPTIONAL READING

**Job 22**

Daniel was another of God's prophets who ministered during the exile in Babylon. The Babylonians employed a process of assimilation whereby young people held in captivity were trained to serve in the king's court. Daniel was one of these young men, but the actions he took in Daniel 1–2 show he had no plan to assimilate into Babylonian faith. Daniel and his three friends disciplined themselves to eat only vegetables and drink water so as not to compromise their faithfulness to God in the matter of dietary laws. God gave the faithful young men knowledge, understanding, and wisdom, enabling them to serve with wisdom.

**Daniel's story is one that details what faithfulness looks like during a time of hardship. Where did you see examples of Daniel's faithfulness? In your own life, where do you see examples of your own faithfulness?**

HIGHLIGHT

EXPLAIN

APPLY

RESPOND

WEEK 43

# 211//DANIEL 2

MEMORY VERSE

**Daniel 3:17-18**

OPTIONAL READING

**Job 23**

The dream Daniel interpreted in Daniel 2 focused on kingdoms: the power of Nebuchadnezzar's kingdom and a future greater kingdom that would never end. In an account reminiscent of that of Joseph, this interpretation was purely supernatural—not only did Daniel give an interpretation of the dream, but he retold the dream itself. The interpretation Daniel gave, which came from the Lord, was looking to Jesus Christ, who would institute a new kingdom and whose reign would never end. From the beginning of this prophetic book, we see that God's people can trust in God's power and control along with the goodness of His Word.

**What does it look like for you to have the same faith that Daniel had in God when facing an uncertain future? How does this compare with your present level of faith?**

HIGHLIGHT

EXPLAIN

APPLY

RESPOND

# 212//DANIEL 3

MEMORY VERSE
**Daniel 3:17-18**

OPTIONAL READING
**Job 24**

Daniel 3 records a well-known event of three Jewish men—Shadrach, Meshach, and Abednego—who refused to compromise their faith in God. Nebuchadnezzar made a statue and demanded that all his subjects bow down and worship it. To refuse to worship the statue meant disobeying the king's decree, which was considered paramount to disobeying the king himself. Shadrach, Meshach, and Abednego meant no disrespect to the king. Their failure to bow down to the gold statue was motivated by their own faith relationship with the One true God. The determined faith of Shadrach, Meshach, and Abednego was matched only by Nebuchadnezzar's rage at their refusal to obey him. In the heat of his anger, he ordered the men to be thrown into a furnace of fire, but when the men were thrown into the fire, the men remained untouched. Nebuchadnezzar witnessed firsthand God's presence with His servants in the fiery furnace, and the men emerged unscathed.

**In what situation might God be calling you to take a stand with the same courage as Shadrach, Meshach, and Abednego? Take some time to reflect on the truths about God and the expectations of His followers that are revealed through Daniel 3. In what ways have you claimed God's glory as your own?**

HIGHLIGHT

EXPLAIN

APPLY

RESPOND

MEMORY VERSE

**Daniel 3:17-18**

# 213//DANIEL 4

OPTIONAL READING

**Job 25**

God makes His will known to men—whether they believe in Him or not. When Daniel boldly spoke truth to Nebuchadnezzar, he was delivering some absurd—and bad news. But when the events of the dream (and the reality of its interpretation) came to pass, the end result was this pagan king being forced to bow down to the holy God. In this chapter, we are reminded that God is present with His people in every threatening situation and uses their faithfulness to glorify His name. Also, we are warned against claiming authority that doesn't belong to us.

**Is there something you're currently facing that you need to get fresh perspective on God's will? Pray for wisdom and discernment as you boldly proclaim the truth of God's Word in that situation.**

HIGHLIGHT

EXPLAIN

APPLY

RESPOND

MEMORY VERSE

**Daniel 3:17-18**

# 214//DANIEL 5

OPTIONAL READING

**Job 26**

In chapter 4, Nebuchadnezzar learned that God alone controls the world; Belshazzar, however, failed to learn from Nebuchadnezzar's example and had his kingdom taken away from him and given to the Medes and Persians. When Daniel was at a feast thrown by the king, Belshazzar saw a vision of a cryptic message written on the wall, which Daniel interpreted, calling out Belshazzar's failure to honor the One true God. At the end of the chapter, after Belshazzar was assassinated, we see yet another changing of power in the land—one which would ultimately test Daniel.

**Belshazzar received a stark, visual sign that God was in control. What signs have you seen in your life that God is in control of everything?**

HIGHLIGHT

EXPLAIN

APPLY

RESPOND

MEMORY VERSE

**Daniel 3:17-18**

# 215//DANIEL 6

OPTIONAL READING

**Job 27**

Because of the interpretive powers Daniel displayed, he was singled out by officials in the court who felt threatened by him, and these men watched Daniel's life for an opportunity to pit him against the king. Knowing Daniel's faith in God, they manipulated the king to sign into law a mandate that forced everyone to pray only to the king, with the punishment of disobedience being death in a lion's den. Daniel courageously maintained his discipline of prayer even though doing so brought a death sentence. When the king found Daniel alive after spending the night in the lion's den, he worshiped God and cast the "wise men" to the lions. As we practice the discipline of prayer, we will grow in our faith in God, trusting that He can help us face any situation with courage. Do not give up on prayer. Prayer will prove to be a lifeline of communication with God.

**Daniel's faith was validated by the intervention of God. How has God proven Himself faithful in your life—even so far today? What impact should this have on your prayer life?**

HIGHLIGHT

EXPLAIN

APPLY

RESPOND

## WEEK 44

# 216//DANIEL 9

MEMORY VERSE

**Daniel 9:4-5**

OPTIONAL READING

**Job 28**

In addition to demonstrating a life of faithfulness to God through strenuous circumstances, the Book of Daniel also includes several chapters of prophecy concerning end times events. As these prophetic visions of judgment and tribulation unfolded, Daniel prayed for God's forgiveness, repeatedly confessing the sins of the people before Him. Daniel's life was marked by strict devotion to God, His will, and His Word, even while in the grips of the Babylonian captivity. In turn, God used him to deliver a message of hope for His people to all who had ears to hear it.

**What role has repeated confession of sin played in your life? What does confessing your sin before God do to your heart?**

HIGHLIGHT

EXPLAIN

APPLY

RESPOND

MEMORY VERSE

Daniel 9:4-5

# 217//DANIEL 10

OPTIONAL READING

Job 29

Few people in history have gotten a glimpse of the things that Daniel got to see. Chapter 10 details Daniel's final vision, which he received in the third year of Cyrus, the Persian conqueror of Babylon. In this vision, Daniel sees a supernatural being clothed in linen and covered in stunning beauty which Daniel can only relate through metaphor. Though the message he was delivering concerning a coming war is detailed in the next chapter, this chapter reminds us of an active supernatural realm all around us—much like the revelation during Elisha's time of a supernatural army surrounding God's faithful servants (2 Kings 6).

**How does the understanding that there are forces beyond what we can see affect you in your everyday life?**

HIGHLIGHT

EXPLAIN

APPLY

RESPOND

MEMORY VERSE

**Daniel 9:4-5**

# 218//DANIEL 12

OPTIONAL READING

**Job 30**

Among the specific things God revealed to Daniel was a time of international turmoil that resulted in the persecution and death of some of His people. There is hope, though, and the time of conflict in persecution will come to an end with the vindication of the righteous. Eternal life awaits those whose names are found written in the book, but eternal shame for those who rebelled against God. This eternal life—secured for us through the sacrificial life, death, and resurrection of Jesus—is the source of ultimate hope and confidence for every believer of Christ. We know that Jesus will come again and make eternal life in the presence of God our eternal reality, and until then, we are to live out our mission of being His disciples in a lost and hopeless world.

**Where is your greatest hope invested? Is it in a job? In a relationship? Ask the Lord to show you where you are placing your hope and to lead you to hope in Christ above all things.**

HIGHLIGHT

EXPLAIN

APPLY

RESPOND

MEMORY VERSE

**Daniel 9:4-5**

# 219//EZRA 1

OPTIONAL READING

**Job 31**

Just as God brought destruction upon the city of Jerusalem through the destruction of the temple of the Lord, so He brought about the eventual restoration of the temple and the return of the exiles as recorded in Ezra. For the first period of the Israelites' return to the city, the Lord spoke to Cyrus, the king of Persia, who also happened to be a Gentile non-believer. It was through Cyrus that the Lord made the return of His people possible. Cyrus offered reentry into the land to anyone who would help rebuild the temple, to which he was also going to restore all of the treasures stolen from the original temple by Nebuchadnezzar.

**When have you seen someone be used as in instrument of God without them knowing it?**

HIGHLIGHT

EXPLAIN

APPLY

RESPOND

MEMORY VERSE

**Daniel 9:4-5**

# 220//EZRA 2

OPTIONAL READING

**Job 32**

The Lord's divine plan is evident through both the exile and return of the people to Jerusalem. This is especially evident in His use of Cyrus to be an instrument for His divine will. Even a Persian king recognized the power, control, and sovereignty of the God of the universe. Like the Jews who responded to the opportunity, we should respond with joy, gratitude, and determination to the opportunities God gives us to be a part of His work also.

**How have you seen God work in unexpected ways in and around you lately? How can you use that remembrance as motivation to serve Him this week?**

HIGHLIGHT

EXPLAIN

APPLY

RESPOND

WEEK 45

# 221//EZRA 3

MEMORY VERSE

**Ezra 6:22**

OPTIONAL READING

**Job 33**

Just months after leaving Babylon, the exiles had rebuilt the altar and restored the formal forms of worship given through Moses. They also hired laborers and purchased building materials so the temple could be rebuilt. The Lord's help was evident in laying the temple's foundation, and they used that as an opportunity for worship and to bring glory to His name. This caused the Jews to praise God by declaring His essential character. Their joy came because they seized the opportunity God gave to participate in His work. But credit for the work's success was due to God, not the people.

**What lessons for your own life can you learn from the picture of the people's worship in this text?**

HIGHLIGHT

EXPLAIN

APPLY

RESPOND

MEMORY VERSE

**Ezra 6:22**

OPTIONAL READING

**Job 34**

# 222//EZRA 4

Soon after the exiles arrived in Jerusalem, word of their endeavor reached people living near the ruined city, and opposition to the rebuilding efforts quickly arose. People approached Zerubbabel with an offer of help, but in reality, they opposed the Jewish effort and intended to sabotage it. This opposition brought construction to a standstill, and nothing proceeded for well over a decade. Despite our faithfulness to God, we are guaranteed opposition to His work in the world. As this part of God's story reminds us, opposition cannot hinder God's faithfulness to His people or His purposes.

**How does the expectation of opposition to God's work affect the mentality you have for doing it faithfully?**

HIGHLIGHT

EXPLAIN

APPLY

RESPOND

MEMORY VERSE

**Ezra 6:22**

OPTIONAL READING

**Job 35**

# 223//EZRA 5

Finally, after more than a decade, construction resumed on the temple, but the building activity in Jerusalem raised suspicion among local Persian officials. But when they were investigated, those doing the construction relayed a message to King Darius that communicated they had approval to build. Even years later, one decision made by a former king, inspired by God, continued to reap benefits for God's people.

**What is something you can set in motion today that will pay spiritual dividends later?**

HIGHLIGHT

EXPLAIN

APPLY

RESPOND

MEMORY VERSE

**Ezra 6:22**

OPTIONAL READING

**Job 36**

# 224//EZRA 6

Discovery of Cyrus' decree from years ago ensured the completion of the temple. When restoration of the temple was complete, the people participated in Passover, which marked the renewal of religious life for the Jews, who could once again worship in obedience to God's Word. The restored exiles had many reasons for being joyful. Primarily, the Lord made them joyful because the Persian king's attitude had changed. We, too, should rejoice in a God who directs the decrees of human kings. Since the time of the garden of Eden when sin entered the world, God has been about the business of restoring His people to Himself, and He continues to do so today. At the heart of our restoration is repentance of sin and obedience to Him.

**What are some ways you can express joy and gratitude to God for providing salvation in Jesus Christ? How can you live in a way that compels others to do the same?**

HIGHLIGHT

EXPLAIN

APPLY

RESPOND

# 225//ZECHARIAH 2

**MEMORY VERSE**
**Ezra 6:22**

**OPTIONAL READING**
**Job 37**

Zechariah was one of God's prophets appointed to deliver His messages to the Jews who returned to Jerusalem after the exile. One of the reasons God sent Zechariah was to encourage the people to continue their work on the temple even in the face of opposition. Through a series of eight visions to Zechariah, God revealed His purposes to His people. He would restore their city and their relationship with Him, and eventually, He would give Israel final victory over its enemies.

**God brings peace and hope at the most unexpected times and in the most unexpected ways. When do you feel most at peace?**

HIGHLIGHT

EXPLAIN

APPLY

RESPOND

WEEK 46

# 226//ZECHARIAH 12

MEMORY VERSE

**Ezra 7:10**

OPTIONAL READING

**Job 38**

By the end of the Book of Zechariah, we see a glimpse of God's promise of a Messiah and His promise to pour out the Spirit of grace and prayer on the people of Jerusalem. The prophecies in this book point to Jesus—the One who was pierced on the cross for the sins of mankind, and the One through whom final victory against sin and death is accomplished. Zechariah also prophesied regarding the coming of the Holy Spirit, which took place after Jesus' resurrection and ascension. As believers, we can rejoice that salvation in Christ brings peace today and hope for eternal peace tomorrow. Salvation is made possible through the suffering of the Messiah.

**What are some ways you can express joy as you experience the peace and hope that the Lord's salvation brings? What might be the result as you do?**

HIGHLIGHT

EXPLAIN

APPLY

RESPOND

# 227//EZRA 7

MEMORY VERSE

**Ezra 7:10**

OPTIONAL READING

**Job 39**

Ezra, the scribe we've encountered before (even outside of the book bearing his name), received a special privilege late in his ministry. When the second group of exiles from Babylon were returning to Jerusalem, he got to lead them back himself. He had lived as an exile in Babylon, and longed above all else to see his homeland again. We are told that he acted faithfully and had dedicated his life to studying God's Law, to obey it, and to teach it to those around him.

**What role does God's Word play in your life? What would it look like in your life to devote more time to studying, obeying, and teaching His Word?**

HIGHLIGHT

EXPLAIN

APPLY

RESPOND

# 228//EZRA 8

MEMORY VERSE

**Ezra 7:10**

OPTIONAL READING

**Job 40**

A new Persian king, Artaxerxes I, finally gave Ezra permission to lead a delegation of exiles back home. Their task was to reestablish proper worship of "the God of heaven." God's providential hand appeared in every act leading to the return of His people and the restoration of the nation. God not only used faithful believers like Ezra, but also moved pagan rulers like Artaxerxes to participate in His plan. Ezra wanted to implement a spiritual revival in Israel based on God's Word. God's people were meant to lead the way in demonstrating what life can be like when lived in accordance with God and His Word. Today, we have the opportunity to obey God and to show a lost world how abundant life can be through faith in Jesus Christ and faithfulness to God's Word.

**What does your present level of dedication to God's Word say about the degree to which you treasure and rely on it? What can you do to make it a more central part of your life?**

HIGHLIGHT

EXPLAIN

APPLY

RESPOND

MEMORY VERSE

**Ezra 7:10**

OPTIONAL READING

**Job 41**

# 229//EZRA 9

After settling into Jerusalem, Ezra received an official report on affairs in Judah, but the news was devastating. Instead of living as God's chosen and set apart people, men had married foreign wives, which was in direct opposition to God's command. This issue was not one of race or nationalism; it was a spiritual problem because the women worshiped false gods. Casual acceptance of these religions by husbands denied the Lord's claim that He alone was God. Consequently, the nation the Lord commanded to be holy had become no different from its pagan neighbors. Ezra grieved over how far God's people had fallen, and he did it publicly—an action that would soon reap enormous spiritual benefit in the lives of God's people.

**Look at the current spiritual state of your life. Is it something to rejoice in or grieve over? What is an action that you need to take as a result of this evaluation?**

HIGHLIGHT

EXPLAIN

APPLY

RESPOND

# 230//EZRA 10

**MEMORY VERSE**
**Ezra 7:10**

**OPTIONAL READING**
**Job 42**

As a result of Ezra's public confession, revival broke out. Suddenly, all across Israel, the people individually and collectively renewed their covenant with God. Like Ezra, we need to be people who are grieved over the presence of sin in our lives and the lives of our loved ones. God has chosen us and set us apart for His glory to be lights for Him in our world. Only with a healthy view of our sin can we live the life of repentance and obedience to God that He calls us to live for our own good and His glory.

**Read 1 Peter 1:13-16. How are you doing at living set apart for God? What is one area of your life in which you need a greater reliance on Him to enable you to pursue holiness?**

HIGHLIGHT

EXPLAIN

APPLY

RESPOND

WEEK 47

# 231//ESTHER 1

MEMORY VERSE
**Esther 4:14**

OPTIONAL READING
**Lamentations 1**

Esther is one of the most unusual and remarkable books in the entire Old Testament. It is the only book in Scripture that never mentions God, even though His presence is apparent on every page. The events it describes cover a 10-year period during the reign of Xerxes I, also known here as Ahasuerus. He was an arrogant ruler, drunk with power, who revealed his propensity for rash action by deposing the queen for refusing him.

**Where have you seen God work and move even in situations where He is not expressly acknowledged? What does this tell you about His sovereignty?**

HIGHLIGHT

EXPLAIN

APPLY

RESPOND

**MEMORY VERSE**
Esther 4:14

**OPTIONAL READING**
Lamentations 2

# 232//ESTHER 2

After Ahasuerus deposed the queen, he launched an empire-wide search for a new queen that lasted four years. Eventually, a woman named Esther was brought in as a part of this search. Esther's story represents a clear picture of God's providential protection and care of His covenant people. Esther was a Jew who God placed in a position to influence the destiny of His people and nations at a time when they would need an advocate. Even in our most trying situations, God is always at work for our long-term good, even if in the short-term it is not clear how He's doing so. He wants His people to trust Him wholeheartedly and confidently—even in the midst of radical, unexpected change.

**What is one unexpected situation you are currently facing? Based on your reading of Esther, what are some applications you've learned that will help you know you can trust God completely during this situation? How should this change the way you respond to it?**

HIGHLIGHT

EXPLAIN

APPLY

RESPOND

MEMORY VERSE

**Esther 4:14**

# 233//ESTHER 3

OPTIONAL READING

**Lamentations 3**

Esther reads like a modern-day political thriller. In chapter 3, the plot thickens with the introduction of the villain, a man named Haman who had a powerful position in the king's court. Haman descended from a Canaanite tribe who consistently opposed Israel, from the exodus out of Egypt to the reign of David. When Mordecai failed to show Haman the respect he desired, he determined to eliminate all the Jews from the empire. Haman persuaded King Ahasuerus that the Jews threatened the Persian empire's national security. As a result, he obtained a royal decree, setting aside a time for slaughtering the Jewish people. God had placed Esther in a situation in which she could make an astounding difference so long as she trusted Him.

**Are you currently in the middle of something where you feel God has placed you for a specific purpose? What is it? How can you act faithfully in this situation?**

HIGHLIGHT

EXPLAIN

APPLY

RESPOND

MEMORY VERSE

**Esther 4:14**

# 234//ESTHER 4

OPTIONAL READING

**Lamentations 4**

Mordecai challenged Esther with the truth that God had a specific purpose in placing her in her royal position. God will not fail to keep His promises or fall short of His purposes. Therefore, the deliverance of the Jews was certain. The only question was what Esther's role in that deliverance would be. God had made her queen so that she could deliver His people through her position and His provision. Esther's account serves as a reminder that God places people where they can serve Him.

**What do you learn about trusting God from Esther 3–4? How should this change the way you view your earthly positions of responsibility, power, or influence as opportunities to care for God's people and glorify Him?**

HIGHLIGHT

EXPLAIN

APPLY

RESPOND

MEMORY VERSE

**Esther 4:14**

# 235//ESTHER 5

OPTIONAL READING

**Lamentations 5**

Esther finally saw the perfect opportunity to intervene for her people. The stakes were high and the risks were great—she was queen specifically because Ahasuerus had deposed the previous queen for standing up to him. But, after three days of praying and fasting, Esther seized this opportunity with boldness, knowing that whatever came of her request—whether it was success or failure—was the will of the Lord.

**How does knowing the outcome of our steps of faith is in the hands of the Lord bring you comfort?**

HIGHLIGHT

EXPLAIN

APPLY

RESPOND

WEEK 48

# 236//ESTHER 6

MEMORY VERSE
**Ecclesiastes 2:24**

OPTIONAL READING
**Ecclesiastes 1**

In a turn of events that can only be described as an act of God, Haman, this story's villain, sees his plans for evil thwarted. The irony of the situation is on full display: he sought to kill Mordecai, but in a dramatic flair inspired by his own pride, he actually described the way in which Mordecai was to be honored. Mordecai and Esther played no part in this turn of events; it was entirely in the hands of the Lord, who demonstrated He was still the God about whom Joseph said, "You planned evil against me; God planned it for good to bring about the present result—the survival of many people" (Gen. 50:20).

**What is an example of a bad situation that turned out to be something God used to make His glory known?**

HIGHLIGHT

EXPLAIN

APPLY

RESPOND

MEMORY VERSE
**Ecclesiastes 2:24**

# 237//ESTHER 7

OPTIONAL READING
**Ecclesiastes 2**

Just as the honor Haman had planned for himself was showered on Mordecai, the death he'd planned for Mordecai ended up being his own. Throughout all the irony, we are reminded of God's sovereign control over the details of our lives. As you reflect on the picture of God so far in this story, remember that God is in control of your life, which means you can trust Him wholeheartedly.

**Read Psalm 33:12-22. How does the truth of this passage, which we see at work in Esther's life, give you comfort?**

HIGHLIGHT

EXPLAIN

APPLY

RESPOND

MEMORY VERSE

**Ecclesiastes 2:24**

# 238//ESTHER 8

OPTIONAL READING

**Ecclesiastes 3**

Esther exposed Haman's plot, which led Ahasuerus to have him executed, but the edict to kill the Jews remained in effect. Under Persian law, Ahasuerus could not revoke it. Instead, the king issued a second edict authorizing Jews to arm and defend themselves, unleashing two days of violence as the two sides fought openly in its streets and fields. In this chapter, we see Esther's grace and wisdom—she never contradicted the law of the land, but she also never turned from her devotion to God. This kind of wisdom is the wisdom that comes from God, for in it, He is the One who receives all of the glory.

**What is something you need God's wisdom to navigate today? Spend some time in prayer asking God to give you His wisdom and protection.**

HIGHLIGHT

EXPLAIN

APPLY

RESPOND

MEMORY VERSE

**Ecclesiastes 2:24**

# 239//ESTHER 9

OPTIONAL READING

**Ecclesiastes 4**

Following the king's second decree, the Jews overcame their opposition, and afterwards, Mordecai ordered a celebration of these victories, which led to the establishment of the annual Festival of Purim. Because of the faithfulness of Esther and Mordecai, the Jewish people were protected, and God received the glory for everything He had done. Although the name of God is never explicitly mentioned in Esther, the book emphasizes the providence of God, the power of prayer and fasting, and the persuasive potential of courageous men and women of faith. God used Esther and Mordecai in a mighty way to preserve His covenant people—and with them, His ultimate plan of deliverance that would come nearly five centuries later in Jesus Christ.

**Purim was a festival that celebrated God's protection and provision in the lives of His people. Is there an annual day of celebration you should set aside to celebrate a way God has moved mightily in your life?**

HIGHLIGHT

EXPLAIN

APPLY

RESPOND

# 240//ESTHER 10

**MEMORY VERSE**
**Ecclesiastes 2:24**

**OPTIONAL READING**
**Ecclesiastes 5**

Mordecai rose to the second most powerful position in the entire empire. But unlike the king he served under, he used his position to ensure prosperity, good treatment, and positive reputations for all of his descendants. Some of us are in positions of similar influence—and even if we are not, we have influence in a number of different areas. Like Mordecai, we can use our influence for the good of people and the glory of God.

**What can you do today to improve someone else's situation?**

HIGHLIGHT

EXPLAIN

APPLY

RESPOND

WEEK 49

# 241//NEHEMIAH 1

MEMORY VERSE
**Ecclesiastes 8:10**

OPTIONAL READING
**Ecclesiastes 6**

The Book of Nehemiah picks up where Ezra left off in the historical records of the restoration of Jerusalem. Under Ezra's spiritual leadership, the Jews began to renew their allegiance to God, but there was another problem—Jerusalem itself was in shambles, and the people there were greatly grieved because of it. This weighed heavily on the heart of Nehemiah, the cupbearer to Artaxerxes. Nehemiah greatly desired to return to Jerusalem to rebuild the city's wall.

**What is your greatest desire? Have you brought it before God?**

HIGHLIGHT

EXPLAIN

APPLY

RESPOND

MEMORY VERSE
**Ecclesiastes 8:10**

# 242//NEHEMIAH 2

OPTIONAL READING
**Ecclesiastes 7**

Because of his good relationship with the king, Nehemiah was granted the request to return to Jerusalem to begin the project of rebuilding the defensive wall that surrounded the city. But as we will see, the problem with Jerusalem wasn't necessarily the state of its structures, it was the state of its people. The true problem was people who had a disconnected relationship with God. Nehemiah was called to rebuild a city and a community of people in shambles. Because of the exile, Jerusalem was in need of both physical and spiritual renewal. The same is true of our broken world. There are hurting and helpless people all around us—people who need the hope of Christ. When we let this reality sink in, like Nehemiah, we are compelled to step up and make a difference.

**How might you make an impact on the brokenness you encounter on a daily basis?**

HIGHLIGHT

EXPLAIN

APPLY

RESPOND

MEMORY VERSE
**Ecclesiastes 8:10**

# 243//NEHEMIAH 3

OPTIONAL READING
**Ecclesiastes 8**

The work to which God called Nehemiah wasn't easy—and he could not do it alone. One reason the work progressed so quickly was that everyone took part, from rulers and temple personnel, to merchants and citizens with their families. Even the people from the villages who lived a long way from Jerusalem helped. By rallying people from all over, Nehemiah was able to see significant progress.

**How do you rely on the people around you? Why is it better to work together rather than alone?**

HIGHLIGHT

EXPLAIN

APPLY

RESPOND

MEMORY VERSE
**Ecclesiastes 8:10**

# 244//NEHEMIAH 4

OPTIONAL READING
**Ecclesiastes 9**

Not everyone was happy with Nehemiah's plan. In the Persian bureaucracy, lines of authority were not always clear, and some government officials feared that a stronger Jerusalem would diminish their prestige. For others, the development awakened ancient rivalries with the Jews. These enemies would seek to undermine Nehemiah with false accusations and duplicity. As a result, many people living in the vicinity were determined to spoil Nehemiah's plans. When we commit to faithfully serving God, He gives us big, God-sized goals to accomplish—goals that are only possible when we depend on Him. Often times, the bigger the goal, the bigger the opposition and challenges we face. No matter the source of our opposition, God gives us the strength to persevere and remain obedient to our tasks, as Nehemiah and the people of Jerusalem demonstrated for us.

**Are there areas where you are feeling opposition? How does Nehemiah's example speak to you?**

HIGHLIGHT

EXPLAIN

APPLY

RESPOND

MEMORY VERSE

**Ecclesiastes 8:10**

# 245//NEHEMIAH 5

OPTIONAL READING

**Ecclesiastes 10**

During the building program, Nehemiah learned of social injustice among the Jewish population. The number of workers needed for rebuilding Jerusalem's wall was immense. The danger of attack required an equal number of men for military service. The economic strain created by the diversion of so many able-bodied workers from the regular labor force created an opportunity for corruption. Some Jews took advantage of other Jews to increase their profits. Nehemiah knew that the wall would not be completed unless the needs of the people were met. But more importantly, he knew that the rebuilding of the "spiritual city" would never be completed unless he faced the issues at hand.

**Where do you see injustice and corruption around you? What role can you play in addressing it?**

HIGHLIGHT

EXPLAIN

APPLY

RESPOND

WEEK 50

# 246//NEHEMIAH 6

MEMORY VERSE
**Zephaniah 3:17**

OPTIONAL READING
**Ecclesiastes 11**

Despite external opposition and internal problems, the people continued to build the wall. Finally, the work was finished. It had taken only 52 days. From the beginning, Nehemiah had put the matter of rebuilding Jerusalem's wall in God's hands. God's people had determined that the best answer to their opposition was to keep working and to fulfill God's will. As they did so, neighboring nations saw God's power at work in them. When God's people accomplish His work in His strength, God gets the glory.

**What is the greatest obstacle standing in the way of you taking on problems in the world like Nehemiah did? How could doing so enable you to seek justice, love kindness, and walk humbly before your God (Mic. 6:8) as you address people's deepest spiritual needs by pointing them to Christ? How do you need to rely on Him to make this possible?**

HIGHLIGHT

EXPLAIN

APPLY

RESPOND

# 247//NEHEMIAH 7

**MEMORY VERSE**
**Zephaniah 3:17**

**OPTIONAL READING**
**Ecclesiastes 12**

Nehemiah 7 and 8 represent beautiful points in the story of the rebuilding of Jerusalem's walls. First, the finished city needed people to populate it. So we see in a moment marked by new gatekeepers, musicians, and priests, the long-awaited return of Jewish exiles into the crown jewel of their faith. Additionally, after rooting out corruption and injustice, Nehemiah put his brother Hanani in charge of the city for a specific reason: "he was a faithful man who feared God more than most" (7:2).

**Why are those who are faithful and God-fearing the people you want in positions of leadership?**

HIGHLIGHT

EXPLAIN

APPLY

RESPOND

# 248//NEHEMIAH 8

MEMORY VERSE

**Zephaniah 3:17**

OPTIONAL READING

**Zephaniah 1**

The building was complete, the people returned, all that was left was the coming, inevitable spiritual revival to match the physical revival already accomplished. So Nehemiah brought in Ezra the scribe to devote a day for the people to hear the Word of God. Through Scripture, God reveals who He is and what a life lived in obedience to Him looks like. Scripture also provides countless stories of people who have gone before us in the faith and how God has proven faithful to His people time and again. The most important thing we learn through Scripture, though, is the one big story it tells—the story of God's work to redeem His people and to draw them back to Him, which He accomplishes through the death, resurrection, and final victory of Jesus.

**The events described in Nehemiah 1–7 led to celebration and revival among the people. How do the values and comforts of the world threaten to make you complacent in your relationship with God? What can you do this week to combat that temptation?**

HIGHLIGHT

EXPLAIN

APPLY

RESPOND

MEMORY VERSE
**Zephaniah 3:17**

# 249//NEHEMIAH 9

OPTIONAL READING
**Zephaniah 2**

As the Israelites heard the Word of God read to them, they were reminded of God's faithfulness to His people and His plans, but they were also reminded of their unfaithfulness to Him. The sins of their ancestors were responsible for God's judgment against Jerusalem, which is what landed them in exile and necessitated the reconstruction of the city to begin with. Among the things Ezra's reading brought to light was the need for confession and repentance. Jesus once said, "Unless you repent, you will all perish as well" (Luke 13:3,5). Repentance can be defined as a heartfelt sorrow for sin, a renouncing of that sin, and a sincere commitment to turn from it and walk in obedience to Christ. Even as Christians, we often stumble away from the Lord by pursuing less than godly endeavors. We must accept responsibility for wandering away from God. No matter how badly we have sinned, God invites us to return to Him.

**What does the prayer recorded in Nehemiah 9:5-37 reveal about God? What does it remind you about your relationship with Him and the sins of which you need to repent?**

HIGHLIGHT

EXPLAIN

APPLY

RESPOND

# 250//NEHEMIAH 10

**MEMORY VERSE**
**Zephaniah 3:17**

**OPTIONAL READING**
**Zephaniah 3**

Nehemiah 9 involved a time of worship and confession, and it ended by mentioning a covenant the people made with God in light of His provisions and their repentance. The people's covenant with God expressed their commitment to living in obedience to Him and His laws. After renewing their commitment to obey God and His laws, chapter 10 includes several specific promises the people made to show how they would live out this commitment in daily life. The promises, which cover everything from Sabbath practices to sacrifice rituals and tithing, reinforce the idea that God has set apart the Israelites to be His chosen people, and as such, they are to live holy and set apart lives for Him. Similarly, God calls us to live holy and set apart lives, which we do when we live in obedience to Him, pursue Christ, and allow the Holy Spirit to transform us. As God's chosen people today, we are to continue to live as a light for Him in our dark and broken world.

**Read 1 Peter 1:13-16. How do these verses help you better understand God's expectations for His people?**

HIGHLIGHT

EXPLAIN

APPLY

RESPOND

WEEK 51

# 251//NEHEMIAH 11

MEMORY VERSE
**Habakkuk 2:4**

OPTIONAL READING
**Haggai 1**

After the work of rebuilding the wall was completed, God called certain people to relocate their families to Jerusalem and serve Him there. For most people, it meant relocating their families from the surrounding villages and uprooting their lives. Nehemiah instructed the people to cast lots to determine which families should go. Nehemiah 11 teaches that where you live and work matters to God. He has placed His people in specific places around specific people in order to serve Him uniquely. In his letter to the Colossian believers, Paul wrote, "Whatever you do, do it from the heart, as something done for the Lord and not for people" (Col. 3:23). This verse reminds us that, for the Christian, all of life is about glorying God and serving Him—there should no distinction between your secular duty and your sacred duty. Our attitude toward work makes a great deal of difference. As Christians, we can and should add an eternal dimension to our viewpoint. We know our ultimate reward for a job well done will come from the Lord.

**Think about where you live and where you work. What does your mission field look like? What needs are there? How might God have placed you uniquely there to fulfill those needs through Him?**

HIGHLIGHT

EXPLAIN

APPLY

RESPOND

MEMORY VERSE

**Habakkuk 2:4**

# 252//NEHEMIAH 12

OPTIONAL READING

**Haggai 2**

The completion of the wall and the repopulation of the city were celebrated with a dedication of the wall. This celebration included singing, ritual purification, and a procession around the wall that Nehemiah led. The people recognized that their ability to rebuild the wall so quickly amid such opposition was possible only because of God's provision, so they worshiped Him with songs of thanksgiving and praise. The climax of the celebration was the presentation of offerings to Him. We live in a culture that values individualism and a "pull yourself up by the bootstraps" mentality, which hinders us from acknowledging that even our best efforts and accomplishments are the result of God's blessing and provision in our lives. Every gift, talent, and opportunity you have is a result of God's desire to be glorified through your life, which He knows will alone lead to your greatest fulfillment and joy. Think about your offerings—everything from your monetary tithe to the way you spend your talents and time. Are you living like God is the source of everything you have?

**Spend a few minutes celebrating what God has done in your life. What do you recall about Him through this time of reflection? What do you learn about His purpose for your life?**

HIGHLIGHT

EXPLAIN

APPLY

RESPOND

MEMORY VERSE

**Habakkuk 2:4**

# 253//NEHEMIAH 13

OPTIONAL READING

**Song of Solomon 1**

The final chapter of Nehemiah concludes with an update from Nehemiah about what occurred in the newly revived city after he departed. Nehemiah was governor in Jerusalem for 12 years. Upon completing his mission, Nehemiah returned to Babylon to serve King Artaxerxes as he had promised, but soon found himself in the important position of spiritual leader once again, helping the people of God restore their relationship with Him. At its heart, the Book of Nehemiah is about restoration—the restoration of a city and the restoration of the people of God. It begins and ends by challenging us to assess our spiritual lives.

**What have you learned about God, about yourself, and about your own need for restoration as you have read through the Book of Nehemiah?**

HIGHLIGHT

EXPLAIN

APPLY

RESPOND

**MEMORY VERSE**
**Habakkuk 2:4**

**OPTIONAL READING**
**Song of Solomon 2**

# 254//HABAKKUK 1

We have no biographical information about Habakkuk. In fact, less is known about this author than any other biblical writer. Regardless, the thoughts and themes of this book have permeated Christian thought for thousands of years because of how universal—and personal—they feel. Habakkuk 1 is a sort of call and response, a conversation with God, Himself, where Habakkuk asks Him some extremely heavy questions about the nature of justice and the righteousness of God's anger against it.

**Have you ever found yourself asking questions of God like the ones that Habakkuk asked? Which of the questions he asked feels most personal to you? How did God's first answer address that question?**

HIGHLIGHT

EXPLAIN

APPLY

RESPOND

MEMORY VERSE

**Habakkuk 2:4**

# 255//HABBAKKUK 2

OPTIONAL READING

**Song of Solomon 3**

Chapter 2 might be relatively short, but it is heavy. Inside, it describes five woes: lust for control (vv. 6-8), greed and unjust gain (vv. 9-11), violence (vv. 12-14), drunkenness, lust, and corrupting others (vv. 15-17), and idolatry (vv. 18-20). Each of the woes Habakkuk describes—and the manner in which he describes them—highlight what a godly man he was, as he separated himself from others and got away to a quiet place to await God's response. God invites us to approach Him with our questions and struggles as Habakkuk did. He is big enough to handle anything, and is faithful to answer those questions asked from a contrite heart.

**Habakkuk 2:4 is the most famous verse in this book. How does it provide an answer to the questions he has asked?**

HIGHLIGHT

EXPLAIN

APPLY

RESPOND

WEEK 52

# 256//HABAKKUK 3

MEMORY VERSE

**Malachi 3:1**

OPTIONAL READING

**Song of Solomon 4**

The major theme of this book follows Habakkuk's growth from a faith plagued by doubt to a faith rooted in absolute trust in God. This third chapter shows that transformation and paints Habakkuk as a man expressing true faith in God and His plan, even if he doesn't completely understand. He has grown into the kind of man God called righteous in chapter 2: He lives by faith. This same calling has been extended to us repeatedly throughout Scripture, both in the Old Testament and the New (Rom. 1:17; Gal. 3:11; Heb. 10:38), and the same outcome awaits us as awaited Habakkuk. We can grow in our relationship with and understanding of God as we live our lives by faith.

**What does it look like for you to "rejoice in the God of my salvation" (v.18)? Has Habakkuk inspired you to re-evaluate any part of your own personal walk?**

HIGHLIGHT

EXPLAIN

APPLY

RESPOND

MEMORY VERSE

**Malachi 3:1**

# 257//MALACHI 1

OPTIONAL READING

**Song of Solomon 5**

Malachi was the last of the Old Testament prophets. He prophesied at the same time Ezra and Nehemiah were leading God's people. Four centuries of prophetic silence followed his proclamation. The next prophet to speak in Scripture will be John the Baptist. Malachi predicted John's coming and also the coming of Jesus Christ, the Messiah. God's last recorded word through His prophets before the coming of Jesus into the world was for His people to honor Him with their hearts and to serve Him faithfully with their lives. The Book of Malachi begins with an emphasis on the greatness of God as seen in His love for His people in Israel. One of the first issues Malachi raised was God's accusation that Israel's priests disrespected Him by offering defiled sacrifices that were worthless. Those offerings revealed a contemptible attitude toward God. Malachi's warning reminds us that God's greatness requires from us a worthy gift and a loving giver. We need to have a wholehearted love for God and show that love through our actions and through worship that is worthy of His name.

**How might you demonstrate more faithfully your wholehearted love for God?**

HIGHLIGHT

EXPLAIN

APPLY

RESPOND

MEMORY VERSE

**Malachi 3:1**

# 258//MALACHI 2

OPTIONAL READING

**Song of Solomon 6**

In Malachi 2, the prophet addressed specific sins of the priests and the people who were compromising their commitments to God—commitments that God takes very seriously. The priests were to revere God's name, give the people true instructions, live before God in peace and fairness, and turn the people from sin. They had done none of the above. Additionally, the people of Israel were the family of God; instead of honoring their family commitments to God and to one another, they were compromising those commitments by marrying people who worshiped idols and accepting their practices. God rebuked them and threatened to remove them from the community along with rejecting their worship. God has called us all to serve Him in some way. Whatever position or avenue of service you've accepted in response to God's leading is a covenant made with Him. God calls us to live honorably for Him by setting godly examples in our relationships and obligations, and Malachi's words remind us He takes it very seriously—even when we do not.

**If those closest to you followed your example in worship, what would their worship look like? What needs to change in the way you pursue God in worship?**

HIGHLIGHT

EXPLAIN

APPLY

RESPOND

MEMORY VERSE

**Malachi 3:1**

# 259//MALACHI 3

OPTIONAL READING

**Song of Solomon 7**

At the close of Malachi 2, God charged His people with making Him weary by their words. The people charged God with injustice, an accusation that goes against His very character. He also accused them of robbing Him by not giving Him the tithes and offerings He is due. Sometimes we look at the state of the world around us and wonder if anything we do really makes a difference. We can understand where the people of Israel were coming from. They looked at the world around them and saw wicked people prospering, causing them to wonder what benefit there was to serving God. Like the Israelites, we often fail to recognize the goodness of God when things get difficult. It is into that discouraging place that God spoke a word of hope to His people—He would send His messenger (John the Baptist) and then He Himself would come to them and make things right, which He has done through Jesus. Today, as we hold out hope for Jesus' promised return, God still expects His people to remain faithful to Him, which we demonstrate by serving God with right attitudes and right actions.

**What is your own attitude toward serving God? Do you feel that it is worth it to serve God?**

**Are there any attitudes or actions from which these verses are leading you to repent?**

HIGHLIGHT

EXPLAIN

APPLY

RESPOND

MEMORY VERSE

**Malachi 3:1**

# 260//MALACHI 4

OPTIONAL READING

**Song of Solomon 8**

At the close of Malachi's prophecy, God reminded the people that a final day of judgment and blessing was coming. God described this as a day when the wicked (those who did not follow God) would be consumed and the righteous (those who follow God) would be healed and their victory over evil complete. Before that day, Elijah would appear to prepare people for the coming day. About five centuries after Malachi lived, both an angel (Luke 1:16-17) and Jesus (Matt. 17:10-13) confirmed that John the Baptist fulfilled Malachi's prophecy of an Elijah who was to come. John was not Elijah in such a literal sense (John 1:21). Instead, John the Baptist was zealous for the Lord as Elijah was, turned people back to the Lord as Elijah did, and prepared the way for the Lord to come to His people as Elijah exemplified. Tucked into these final verses of the Old Testament is the hope of the gospel. The only thing that could finally preserve people from God's judgment against sin is for Jesus to bear the curse for us. He accomplished this in His death on the cross and in fulfillment of Malachi's prophecy.

**Take some time to reflect on your readings through the Old Testament. Write down some of the truths you have learned about God and ways you have been challenged by seeing His great story of redemption unfold. Then spend some quiet time in prayer.**

HIGHLIGHT

EXPLAIN

APPLY

RESPOND

# SAMPLE HEAR ENTRY

Read: Philippians 4:10-13
Date: 12-22-18
Title: The Secret of Contentment

H // Highlight

"I am able to do all things through him who strengthens me" (Phil. 4:13).

E // Explain

Paul was telling the church at Philippi that he had discovered the secret of contentment. No matter the situation in Paul's life, he realized that Christ was all he needed, and Christ was the One who strengthened him to persevere through difficult times.

A // Apply

In my life I will experience many ups and downs. My contentment isn't found in circumstances. Rather, it's based on my relationship with Jesus Christ. Only Jesus gives me the strength I need to be content in every circumstance of life.

R // Respond

Lord Jesus, please help me as I strive to be content in You. Through Your strength I can make it through any situation I must face.

# SAMPLE PRAYER LOG

| Date Asked | Prayer Request | Date Answered |
|---|---|---|
| | | |
| | | |
| | | |
| | | |
| | | |
| | | |
| | | |
| | | |
| | | |
| | | |
| | | |
| | | |
| | | |
| | | |

# SAMPLE SCRIPTURE-MEMORY CARD

You, therefore, my son, be strong in the grace that is in Christ Jesus. And what you have heard from me in the presence of many witnesses, commit to faithful men who will be able to teach others also.

**2 Timothy 2:1-2**

# F-260 OT BIBLE-READING PLAN

## WEEK 1

- ☐ Genesis 1
- ☐ Genesis 2
- ☐ Genesis 3
- ☐ Genesis 4
- ☐ Genesis 5

MEMORY VERSE

Psalm 1:1-2

## WEEK 2

- ☐ Genesis 6
- ☐ Genesis 8
- ☐ Genesis 9
- ☐ Genesis 11
- ☐ Genesis 12

MEMORY VERSE

Psalm 6:1-2

## WEEK 3

- ☐ Genesis 15
- ☐ Genesis 16
- ☐ Genesis 17
- ☐ Genesis 18
- ☐ Genesis 19

MEMORY VERSE

Psalm 13:5

## WEEK 4

- ☐ Genesis 20
- ☐ Genesis 21
- ☐ Genesis 22
- ☐ Genesis 24
- ☐ Genesis 25

MEMORY VERSE

Psalm 16:1-2

## WEEK 5

- ☐ Genesis 26
- ☐ Genesis 27
- ☐ Genesis 28
- ☐ Genesis 29
- ☐ Genesis 30

MEMORY VERSE

Genesis 26:3-5

## WEEK 6

- ☐ Genesis 31
- ☐ Genesis 32
- ☐ Genesis 33
- ☐ Genesis 35
- ☐ Genesis 37

MEMORY VERSE

Psalm 27:4

## WEEK 7

- ☐ Genesis 39
- ☐ Genesis 40
- ☐ Genesis 41
- ☐ Genesis 42
- ☐ Genesis 43

MEMORY VERSE

Psalm 31:3

## WEEK 8

- ☐ Genesis 44
- ☐ Genesis 45
- ☐ Genesis 46
- ☐ Genesis 47
- ☐ Genesis 48

MEMORY VERSE

Psalm 40:1-3

## WEEK 9

- ☐ Genesis 49
- ☐ Genesis 50
- ☐ Exodus 1
- ☐ Exodus 2
- ☐ Exodus 3

MEMORY VERSE

Genesis 50:20

## WEEK 10

- ☐ Exodus 4
- ☐ Exodus 5
- ☐ Exodus 6
- ☐ Exodus 7
- ☐ Exodus 8

MEMORY VERSE

Psalm 46:1

## WEEK 11

- ☐ Exodus 9
- ☐ Exodus 10
- ☐ Exodus 11
- ☐ Exodus 12
- ☐ Exodus 13

MEMORY VERSE

Psalm 51:1-2

## WEEK 12

- ☐ Exodus 14
- ☐ Exodus 16
- ☐ Exodus 17
- ☐ Exodus 19
- ☐ Exodus 20

MEMORY VERSE

Psalm 57:2

## WEEK 13

- ☐ Exodus 24
- ☐ Exodus 25
- ☐ Exodus 26
- ☐ Exodus 27
- ☐ Exodus 28

MEMORY VERSE

Psalm 63:1-3

## WEEK 14

- ☐ Exodus 29
- ☐ Exodus 30
- ☐ Exodus 31
- ☐ Exodus 32
- ☐ Exodus 33

MEMORY VERSE

Psalm 68:5

## WEEK 15

- ☐ Exodus 34
- ☐ Exodus 35
- ☐ Exodus 40
- ☐ Leviticus 8
- ☐ Leviticus 9

MEMORY VERSE

Psalm 71:5-6

## WEEK 16

- ☐ Leviticus 16
- ☐ Leviticus 23
- ☐ Leviticus 26
- ☐ Numbers 11
- ☐ Numbers 12

MEMORY VERSE

Psalm 77:11-12

## WEEK 17

- ☐ Numbers 13
- ☐ Numbers 14
- ☐ Numbers 16
- ☐ Numbers 17
- ☐ Numbers 20

MEMORY VERSE

Psalm 84:11

## WEEK 18

- ☐ Numbers 21
- ☐ Numbers 22
- ☐ Numbers 27
- ☐ Numbers 34
- ☐ Numbers 35

MEMORY VERSE

Psalm 86:15

## WEEK 19

- ☐ Deuteronomy 1
- ☐ Deuteronomy 2
- ☐ Deuteronomy 3
- ☐ Deuteronomy 4
- ☐ Deuteronomy 5

MEMORY VERSE

Deuteronomy 1:29-30

## WEEK 20

- ☐ Deuteronomy 6
- ☐ Deuteronomy 7
- ☐ Deuteronomy 8
- ☐ Deuteronomy 9
- ☐ Deuteronomy 30

MEMORY VERSE

Deuteronomy 6:4-5

## WEEK 21

- ☐ Deuteronomy 31
- ☐ Deuteronomy 32
- ☐ Deuteronomy 34
- ☐ Joshua 1
- ☐ Joshua 2

MEMORY VERSES

Joshua 1:8-9

## WEEK 22

- ☐ Joshua 3
- ☐ Joshua 4
- ☐ Joshua 5
- ☐ Joshua 6
- ☐ Joshua 7

MEMORY VERSES

Psalm 107:9

## WEEK 23

- ☐ Joshua 8
- ☐ Joshua 23
- ☐ Joshua 24
- ☐ Judges 2
- ☐ Judges 3

MEMORY VERSES

Joshua 23:14

## WEEK 24

- ☐ Judges 4
- ☐ Judges 6
- ☐ Judges 7
- ☐ Judges 13
- ☐ Judges 14

MEMORY VERSES

Psalm 119:18

## WEEK 25

- ☐ Judges 15
- ☐ Judges 16
- ☐ Ruth 1
- ☐ Ruth 2
- ☐ Ruth 3

MEMORY VERSES

Psalm 119:50

## WEEK 26

- ☐ Ruth 4
- ☐ 1 Samuel 1
- ☐ 1 Samuel 2
- ☐ 1 Samuel 3
- ☐ 1 Samuel 8

MEMORY VERSES

Psalm 119:156

## WEEK 27

- ☐ 1 Samuel 9
- ☐ 1 Samuel 10
- ☐ 1 Samuel 12
- ☐ 1 Samuel 14
- ☐ 1 Samuel 15

MEMORY VERSES

Psalm 127:1

## WEEK 28

- ☐ 1 Samuel 16
- ☐ 1 Samuel 17
- ☐ 1 Samuel 18
- ☐ 1 Samuel 19
- ☐ 1 Samuel 20

MEMORY VERSE

1 Samuel 16:7

## WEEK 29

- ☐ 1 Samuel 21
- ☐ 1 Samuel 22
- ☐ 1 Samuel 23
- ☐ 1 Samuel 24
- ☐ 1 Samuel 25

MEMORY VERSE

Psalm 138:2

## WEEK 30

- ☐ 1 Samuel 28
- ☐ 1 Samuel 31
- ☐ 2 Samuel 1
- ☐ 2 Samuel 3
- ☐ 2 Samuel 5

MEMORY VERSE

Psalm 141:3

## WEEK 31

- ☐ 2 Samuel 6
- ☐ 2 Samuel 7
- ☐ 2 Samuel 9
- ☐ 2 Samuel 11
- ☐ 2 Samuel 12

MEMORY VERSE

Psalm 145:8-9

## WEEK 32

- ☐ 2 Samuel 24
- ☐ 1 Kings 2
- ☐ 1 Kings 3
- ☐ 1 Kings 6
- ☐ 1 Kings 8

MEMORY VERSE

Proverbs 3:5-6

## WEEK 33

- ☐ 1 Kings 11
- ☐ 1 Kings 12
- ☐ 1 Kings 17
- ☐ 1 Kings 18
- ☐ 1 Kings 19

MEMORY VERSES

Proverbs 4:23

## WEEK 34

- ☐ 1 Kings 21
- ☐ 1 Kings 22
- ☐ 2 Kings 2
- ☐ 2 Kings 3
- ☐ 2 Kings 5

MEMORY VERSE

Proverbs 12:11

## WEEK 35

- ☐ 2 Kings 6
- ☐ Jonah 1
- ☐ Jonah 2
- ☐ Jonah 3
- ☐ Jonah 4

MEMORY VERSE

Proverbs 14:7

## WEEK 36

- ☐ Hosea 1
- ☐ Hosea 2
- ☐ Hosea 3
- ☐ Amos 9
- ☐ Joel 1

MEMORY VERSE

Hosea 6:3

## WEEK 37

- ☐ Joel 2
- ☐ Joel 3
- ☐ Isaiah 6
- ☐ Isaiah 9
- ☐ Isaiah 44

MEMORY VERSE

Isaiah 9:6

## WEEK 38

- ☐ Isaiah 45
- ☐ Isaiah 52
- ☐ Isaiah 53
- ☐ Isaiah 65
- ☐ Isaiah 66

MEMORY VERSE

Isaiah 53:6

## WEEK 39

- ☐ Micah 1
- ☐ Micah 5
- ☐ 2 Kings 17
- ☐ 2 Kings 18
- ☐ 2 Kings 19

MEMORY VERSE

Micah 1:3-4

## WEEK 40

- ☐ 2 Kings 20
- ☐ 2 Kings 21
- ☐ 2 Kings 22
- ☐ 2 Kings 23
- ☐ Jeremiah 1

MEMORY VERSE

Jeremiah 1:4-5

## WEEK 41

- ☐ Jeremiah 25
- ☐ Jeremiah 29
- ☐ Jeremiah 32
- ☐ Jeremiah 33
- ☐ Jeremiah 52

MEMORY VERSE

Jeremiah 29:12

## WEEK 42

- ☐ 2 Kings 24
- ☐ 2 Kings 25
- ☐ Ezekiel 36
- ☐ Ezekiel 37
- ☐ Daniel 1

MEMORY VERSE

Ezekiel 36:26-27

## WEEK 43

- ☐ Daniel 2
- ☐ Daniel 3
- ☐ Daniel 4
- ☐ Daniel 5
- ☐ Daniel 6

MEMORY VERSES

Daniel 3:17-18

## WEEK 44

- ☐ Daniel 9
- ☐ Daniel 10
- ☐ Daniel 12
- ☐ Ezra 1
- ☐ Ezra 2

MEMORY VERSES

Daniel 9:4-5

## WEEK 45

- ☐ Ezra 3
- ☐ Ezra 4
- ☐ Ezra 5
- ☐ Ezra 6
- ☐ Zechariah 2

MEMORY VERSE

Ezra 6:22

## WEEK 46

- ☐ Zechariah 12
- ☐ Ezra 7
- ☐ Ezra 8
- ☐ Ezra 9
- ☐ Ezra 10

MEMORY VERSES

Ezra 7:10

## WEEK 47

- ☐ Esther 1
- ☐ Esther 2
- ☐ Esther 3
- ☐ Esther 4
- ☐ Esther 5

MEMORY VERSE

Esther 4:14

## WEEK 48

- ☐ Esther 6
- ☐ Esther 7
- ☐ Esther 8
- ☐ Esther 9
- ☐ Esther 10

MEMORY VERSES

Ecclesiastes 2:24

## WEEK 49

- ☐ Nehemiah 1
- ☐ Nehemiah 2
- ☐ Nehemiah 3
- ☐ Nehemiah 4
- ☐ Nehemiah 5

MEMORY VERSES

Ecclesiastes 8:10

## WEEK 50

- ☐ Nehemiah 6
- ☐ Nehemiah 7
- ☐ Nehemiah 8
- ☐ Nehemiah 9
- ☐ Nehemiah 10

MEMORY VERSE

Zephaniah 3:17

## WEEK 51

- ☐ Nehemiah 11
- ☐ Nehemiah 12
- ☐ Nehemiah 13
- ☐ Habakkuk 1
- ☐ Habakkuk 2

MEMORY VERSE

Habakkuk 2:4

## WEEK 52

- ☐ Habakkuk 3
- ☐ Malachi 1
- ☐ Malachi 2
- ☐ Malachi 3
- ☐ Malachi 4

MEMORY VERSE

Malachi 3:1

# NOTES //

# INDIVIDUAL RESOURCES

## REPLICATE
PODCAST NETWORK

Subscribe to each of our podcasts below and receive weekly episodes that will inspire, encourage, and equip you to make disciples.

## REPLICATE BOOK

The Replicate book is a culmination of over ten years of training leaders to make disciples. This book will not just show you how to make disciples, but how your church can launch a disciplemaking movement!

## CONNECT WITH US

Follow us on social media so we can connect! We want to help you make disciples and hear all that God is doing in and through you!

# FAMILY RESOURCES

We believe that discipleship starts in the home. Our Foundations Series is designed to help your whole family read, memorize, and apply Scripture through our reading plans, memory decks, and journal plans. These resources will help your church and your family get every age on the same page.

## READING PLANS

Whether you are reading through the F260 or NT260, Replicate provides workbooks for adults, teens, and kids that help your family read through the Bible together and discuss it as a family.

## JOURNAL PLANS

Replicate has created multiple resources that will help you journal through the Bible. You can purchase independent journals or a Bible with the journal plan included.

## MEMORIZATION PLANS

Replicate's Memory Decks will help you and your family memorize Scripture together.

***Learn more at Replicate.org/foundations.***

# CHURCH RESOURCES

## DISCIPLESHIP BLUEPRINT:

Are you a church leader who has a passion for discipleship, but needs a simple strategy that would work for your church?

The Discipleship Blueprint provides training sessions to help you develop a holistic and simple discipleship plan that will drive meaningful engagement and help your church grow both in breadth and depth.

***Learn more at replicate.org/training***

## D-GROUP CONFERENCE KITS

Are you wanting to launch D-Groups in your church? The Conference Kits are a turn-key system to provide you with everything you need to host excellent training events for launching and multiplying D-Groups.

***Learn more at replicate.org/conferencekits***

# THE WORD SERIES

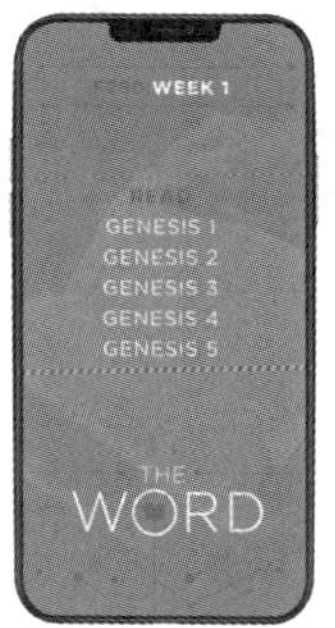

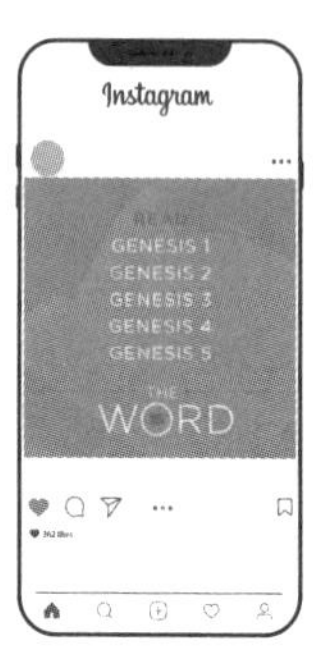

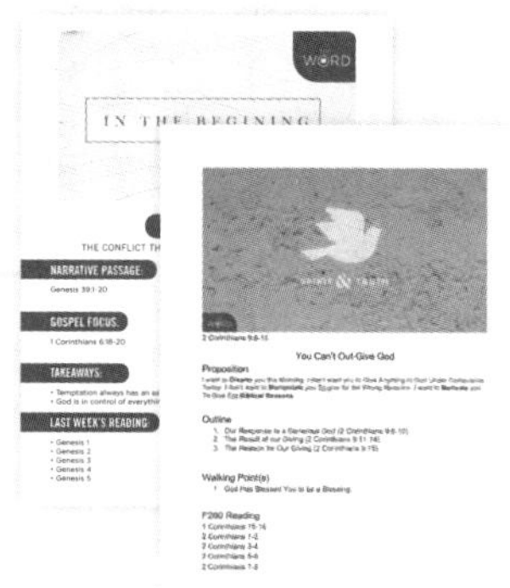


THE WORD Bible Study series takes participants on a journey through the meta-narrative of Scripture from Genesis to Revelation. With 8 series that connect all52 weeks of lessons, your groups will engage with the Word like never before. Additionally, Bible reading plans and H.E.A.R. journaling will allow your whole church to be on the same page throughout the journey.

**THE WORD SERIES INCLUDES:**

- 52 Sermon Templates
- 52 Group Discussion Guides
- Corresponding Adult and Kid Reading Plans
- Bible Reading and Application Framework (H.E.A.R. Journal)
- Weekly Social Media Posts
- 8 Graphic Bundles

***Learn more at replicate.org/WORD***